From : Sam Cassidy – Assistant to Malcolm Tucker [mailto: scassidy@
To : ALL
Subject : Urgent

Has anyone seen Malcolm's briefing folder? If so please return it as a m... ...gency.

Sam Cassidy
On behalf of Malcolm Tucker

****

First published in 2010 by Faber and Faber Ltd., Bloomsbury House, 74–77 Great Russell Street, London WC1B 3DA
Typeset by Faber and Faber Ltd. Printed in Great Britain by Butler Tanner & Dennis Ltd, Frome, Somerset.

A CIP record for this book is available from the British Library.

ISBN 978–0–571–27254–9

10 9 8 7 6 5 4 3 2 1

The Thick of It is a BBC production.

From : Alex Johnson [mailto: ajohnson@gov.org.uk]
To : Malcolm Tucker
Subject : RE : Urgent

Fuck!

From : Martin Spencer [mailto: mspencer@gov.org.uk]
To : Malcolm Tucker
Subject : RE : Urgent

Shit!

From : Melissa Brooks [mailto: mbrooks@gov.org.uk]
To : Malcolm Tucker
Subject : RE : Urgent

FUCKBUCKETS!
Arsepiss! Hope you find it or it's Fuckageddon for all of us.

From : Elaine Horley [mailto: ehorley@gov.org.uk]
To : Malcolm Tucker
Subject : RE : Urgent

It'll be in the last place you think of looking! Always is! Try retracing your steps! Sounds
obvious but it works! ;-)
xxOOxx

From : Glenn Cullen [mailto: glenncullen@dosac.gov.uk]
To : Malcolm Tucker
Subject : RE : Urgent

Did you shove it up Dan Miller's arse? I think you said you were going to shove it up Dan Miller's arse?

From : Terri Coverley [mailto: terricoverley@dosac.gov.uk]
To : Malcolm Tucker
Subject : RE : Urgent

I told you you should be more organised Malcolm. Your 'filing' system was an accident waiting to happen. Maybe my Shoulder Folder Holder wasn't such a ridiculous idea after all?!

From : Dan Miller [mailto: dmiller@gov.org.uk]
To : Malcolm Tucker
Subject : RE : Urgent

Oh dear Malcolm. Oh dear. You do realise this is a very serious breech of security? What am I saying? Of course you realise that. I hope you'll give yourself a very strong talking to and implement the appropriate punishment and won't show yourself any favouritism just because you know you and happen to be you.

From : Cliff Lawton [mailto: clawton@gov.org.uk]
To : Malcolm Tucker
Subject : RE : Urgent

OH HO HO
HAHAHAHAHAHA
HEEHEEHEEHEEHEEHEE

From : Sam Cassidy [mailto: scassidy@gov.org.uk]
To : Malcolm Tucker
Subject :

Spoken to Jo. You definitely didn't leave it at Cabinet.

From : Cliff Lawton [mailto: clawton@gov.org.uk]
To : Malcolm Tucker
Subject : RE : RE: Urgent

RESIGN!

Spoken to Alex. They don't have it at the DTI.

From : Ben Swain
To : Malcolm Tucker
Subject : RE : Urgent

Hi Malcolm.
God, that sounds awful. That must be so … not humiliating, that's not the right word is it? Embarrassing? Excruciating? Maybe I do mean humiliating? Anyway, you shouldn't take it personally. It's the kind of thing that could happen to anyone. And we all understand that. There's a lot of sympathy here for you. A lot of empathy. My heart goes out to you, Malc. I mean, imagine if the press got wind of this. Doesn't bear thinking about. Must be horrible for you. I really really really hope this doesn't turn into a resignation issue for you. You're probably on top of this but have you tried looking in the following? I've made a list of the most embarrassing places it could turn up …

- A bar
- A gay bar
- A brothel
- A gay brothel
- A crack den
- A gay crack den
- The PM's bum hole
- A train
- A plane
- A skip
- A bookies
- A Starbucks
- The reception desk of The Daily Mail
- A British-based Al-Qaeda cell
- Clapham Common

Hope that helps. And very best of luck.

Yours,
Ben

From : Cliff Lawton [mailto: clawton@gov.org.uk]
To : Malcolm Tucker
Subject : RE : RE: RE : Urgent

RESIGN!

From : Sam Cassidy [mailto: scassidy@gov.org.uk]
To : Malcolm Tucker
Subject :

I've made MI5 aware. Spoken to Graham at the House of Commons. They're on the look out.

From : Terri Coverley [mailto: terricoverley@dosac.gov.uk]
To : Malcolm Tucker
Subject : RE : RE : Urgent

Was there anything important in it? Because if it was just receipts and things I wouldn't worry too much.

From : Robert Samson [mailto: rsamson@gov.org.uk]
To : ALL
Subject : RE : Urgent

While we're on the subject of lost property someone has again 'borrowed' the IT department's trolley. Can you please return it. The trolley is vital to the efficient running of the department. This is beyond a joke.

From : Nicola Murray [mailto: nicolamurray@dosac.gov.uk]
To : Malcolm Tucker
Subject : RE : Urgent

Right. Great. I suppose this fucks my Helping Hands policy launch today? Thanks for your helping hands. Which I imagine are now busily employed repeatedly slapping your forehead. You numpty.

From : Robyn Murdoch [mailto: robynmurdoch@dosac.gov.uk]
To : Malcolm Tucker
Subject : RE : Urgent

Don't worry, I'm sure it will turn up! I lost my iPhone in Tesco last week but someone handed it in! How amazing is that?! Have faith – there are still plenty of good guys out there! You just have to work out where they might have handed it in is all. Although, thinking about it, the amount of places you visit that might be tricky. Good luck though!

From : Geoff Holhurst [mailto: gholhurst@gov.org.uk]
To : Malcolm Tucker
Subject : RE : Urgent

Hi Malc,
I'd offer to help look for it but because I have such a tiny head it means my teensy little eyes can't really see anything.

Best of luck though.
Geoff

From : Cliff Lawton [mailto: clawton@gov.org.uk]
To : Malcolm Tucker
Subject : RE : RE : RE : Urgent

RESIGN!

From : Julius Nicholson [mailto: jnicholson@gov.org.uk]
To : ALL
Subject : Lost property

Hello everyone –
A couple of other items appear to have gone missing.
• The party's prospects of winning the election.
• Good practice in government.
• Malcolm's credibility.

If any one recovers any of these items please let me know.
JN

From : Nick Hanway [mailto: nhanway@gov.org.uk]
To : ALL
Subject : Lost property

Shit. This is bigger than when Bob Monkhouse's joke book went missing.

From : Cliff Lawton [mailto: clawton@gov.org.uk]
To : ALL
Subject : RE : Lost property

Even funnier!

From : Jamie MacDonald [mailto: jmacdonald@gov.org.uk]
To : Malcolm Tucker
Subject : Fuckwittery and Arse-twattedness

Alright old man? Got a touch of the old Parkinzheimers? You need me to come over and empty your piss bag? And tie your folders to your sleeves like mittens on string? I can send over some of Tom's medication if you like.

From : Glenn Cullen [mailto: glenncullen@dosac.gov.uk]
To : ALL
Subject : RE : Lost property

Don't know if this helps but ...
I found my thrill on Blueberry Hill.

Have you tried looking on Blueberry Hill?
I'm just throwing it out there ...

From : Alison Foster [mailto: afoster@gov.org.uk]
To : ALL
Subject : Lost property found!

Not Malcolm's folder. But a purse found in the Ladies at lunchtime. Come to my office
B102 to collect.

From : Nick Hanway [mailto: nhanway@gov.org.uk]
To : ALL
Subject : RE : Lost property found!

Oh thank God for that! That is a relief!

From : Cliff Lawton [mailto: clawton@gov.org.uk]
To : Malcolm Tucker
Subject : RE : RE : RE : RE : Urgent

Are you still here?
I thought I told you to RESIGN!

From : Sam Cassidy [mailto: scassidy@gov.org.uk]
To : Malcolm Tucker
Subject :

Looks like you had it with you 'til visiting the DOSAC team at the Watford Business Park for
the Helping Hands pre-brief.

From : Malcolm Tucker [mtucker@gov.org.uk]
To : Oliver Reeder
Subject :

Hello.
I've had sarcastic/ idiotic emails from most of the key figures in your department.
But not you.
You've been very quiet.
Why?

From : Malcolm Tucker [mtucker@gov.org.uk]
To : Oliver Reeder
Subject :

I'm waiting for an answer.

From : Malcolm Tucker [mtucker@gov.org.uk]
To : Oliver Reeder
Subject :

Waiting patiently …

From : Malcolm Tucker [mtucker@gov.org.uk]
To : Oliver Reeder
Subject :

Waiting less patiently …

From : Malcolm Tucker [mtucker@gov.org.uk]
To : Oliver Reeder
Subject :

I'm coming over …

From : Oliver Reeder [mailto: oliverreeder@dosac.gov.uk]
To : Malcolm Tucker
Subject :

Malcolm, hi, yes. So.

Yes, I did have the folder. I found it on a sideboard – you must have forgotten to pick it up between throwing that small chest of drawers at Nicola and storming out. So some kudos there to me for, you know, spotting it and looking after it in that initial period of it being lost.

I was then in the process of bringing it back – again some kudos to me for that too, I think, given how busy/ frantic/ nervous breakdown-y things are with Nicola at the moment. But, unfortunately, Nicola rang me for a moan/ panic/ nervous breakdown and I may (and I stress the word 'may' here) have temporarily mislaid the (already lost) folder en route via our excellent integrated public transport system.

I'm currently trying to retrace my steps in an effort to recover it. Let me assure you that (a) I am giving this my full attention, (b) I didn't read it and am unaware of its contents and (c) I am very, very, very unreservedly, massively sorry.

Yours, with respect and admiration,

Ollie

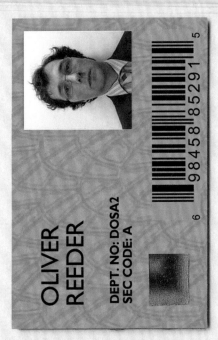

OLIVER REEDER

DEPT. NO: DOSA2
SEC CODE: A

5 98458 85291 6

MALCOLM
TUCKER

DEPT. NO: DOSA2
SEC CODE: A

6 98458 83492 8

ROBYN MURDOCH

DEPT. NO: DOSA2
SEC CODE: A

2 98458 82152 6

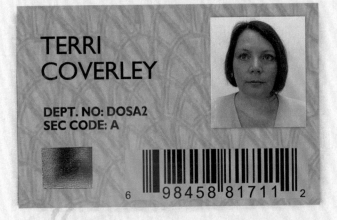

TERRI
COVERLEY

DEPT. NO: DOSA2
SEC CODE: A

6 98458 81711 2

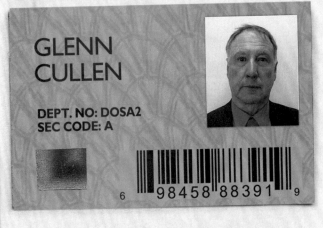

GLENN
CULLEN

DEPT. NO: DOSA2
SEC CODE: A

6 98458 88391 9

BEN
SWAIN

DEPT. NO: DOSA2
SEC CODE: A

6 98458 82796 8

NICOLA
MURRAY

DEPT. NO: DOSA2
SEC CODE: A

6 98458 86482 6

Q&A

My Body & Soul
Nicola Murray

The Minister for the Department of Social Affairs and Citizenship on the pressures of government, her love of the NHS and her wild pot-smoking college days.

Interview by Sophie Heywood.

Nicola Murray, at home in Greater London.
Photograph : Linda McKintosh.

Ever spent a night in hospital? I've got four kids so, yes! And I'm also quite accident-prone! I've been in five car accidents! Although I should add that I was only driving in three of those. And I'm also a hypochondriac. So, yes, I have spent a lot of time in hospital. Luckily for me though this government has done some amazing work investing in hospitals so they're much nicer than they used to be! I sometimes tell people they're now so good they should throw themselves down the stairs just to check them out!! I don't, of course! I'm just having a bit of a fun!

Do you worry about your weight?

I don't know if I would say I worry about my weight. I would say I have 'a real and genuine concern' about my weight. That's a joke! It's the sort of thing politicians say. I don't know if it will come across in print without me doing the voice. But if you could see me and hear me doing the voice – hilarious!

How do you relax?

I find it quite difficult to switch off so I try lots of things. Herbal tea. Rescue remedy. Walking. Meditation. Going to the gym. Listening to classical music - which I hate! Doing the dishes - which I hate! Tidying up - which I hate! Writing to do lists. I also squeeze stress balls. (They don't work!) I drink wine. Plan holidays I will never get to take. Remember fun things I did when I was young. Sometimes I try sucking on a lozenge – don't know why! I used to do yoga but then I broke my sternum. That was another time I had to go to hospital! Which was great in a way because I got to see all the amazing improvements this administration has helped put in place. Although it was very painful. I needed quite a lot of morphine for that one! So I may have slightly hallucinated some of the improvements!

How much sleep do you need?

I need at least six hours a night. I can function on five. Four or less and I feel like a character in Shameless. The problem is I'm a light sleeper and lots of things can wake me up. My husband snoring. Me snoring. My kids snoring. My teeth grinding. The foxes in the garden. The bin men. The cat. The weird noises the house makes like it might suddenly collapse. The dawn chorus. And there's a weird lump on the left side of the bed. And I don't mean my husband! Or do I? No, I'm kidding! I love him to bits. The other thing that keeps me awake, of course, is anxiety about the amount of work we still need to do as a government. Not on the NHS though which is now so good you can cut your own head off, go to A and E and be back at work the next day! I'm not advocating that – it's a joke people!!!

Attitude to smoking?

I think we're over that now aren't we? It just all seems so Eighties. Like Big Audio Dynamite or the Moomins. Or Peter Mannion! Bit of politics! Yes indeed!!!

Attitude to drugs?

It's a complicated issue and I think we have to have a mature attitude to it. I think on the one hand the press tend to be very sensationalist about it as a subject. On the other hand I would never want my kids to get involved in drugs. Having said that I did have a bit of pot when I was at college but who didn't? Having said that, though, if I could go back to when I was a kid I'd tell myself not to do that because I wouldn't be happy with the message it would send to my kids. Mind you, being a kid, I'm not sure I'd have listened to me. I hope I've brought up my kids to know better and to listen to me. I actually didn't like it anyway. It seemed to relax everyone else but, for some reason, it made me very tense.

How do you feel about cosmetic surgery?

What are you saying??!!! I'll have you know in the world of politics I'm bloody good looking! Have you seen Andrew Neil?! He's got a face like a bag of gnocchi.

NHS or private?

NHS of course! You'd expect me to say that and I am saying it but I also mean it. I really do. I love the NHS. It's something we should be very proud of. But people don't tend to get excited about it because when they think of the NHS they think of liquid hand gels and people dying of cancer. But I'm very excited about it. Not about the people dying of cancer. Or actually about the liquid hand gels. But the amazing turnaround in the quality of care is something you just have to see to believe. I've said it before and I'll say it again – get yourself down to your local hospital and check it out you'll be amazed!! They're practically good enough to go on holiday in! That's a light-hearted comment, of course, and not meant to offend people who are in deeply tragic circumstances dealing with terminally-ill loved ones.

Is sex important to you?

Yes! Is that an offer?!!! (I'm joking!!)

Have you ever had therapy?

No. A lot of people tell me I should!!!! But I don't think I need it!

Are you happy?

I'm always happy!! Particularly when I'm in hospital! Particularly when I'm getting really strong drugs! I'm kidding!! Don't do it kids!!!

From : Malcolm Tucker [mailto : mtucker@gov.org.uk]
To : Nicola Murray [mailto : nicolamurray@dosac.gov.uk]
Subject : Press

Oh my god!!! I just read your interview in the Observer!!!!

> From : Nicola Murray [mailto : nicolamurray@dosac.gov.uk]
> To : Malcolm Tucker [mailto : mtucker@gov.org.uk]
> Subject : Re : Press

> Cool! Did you like it?

>> **From :** Malcolm Tucker [mailto : mtucker@gov.org.uk]
>> **To :** Nicola Murray [mailto : nicolamurray@dosac.gov.uk]
>> **Subject : Re : Re : Press**

>> NO.

>>> From : Nicola Murray [mailto : nicolamurray@dosac.gov.uk]
>>> To : Malcolm Tucker [mailto : mtucker@gov.org.uk]
>>> Subject : Re : Re : Re : Press

>>> I thought it made me sound like a human being?

>>>> **From :** Malcolm Tucker [mailto : mtucker@gov.org.uk]
>>>> **To :** Nicola Murray [mailto : nicolamurray@dosac.gov.uk]
>>>> **Subject : Re : Re : Re : Re : Press**

>>>> Yeah like a human being who is deeply mental. You sound like Courtney Love
>>>> on a bungee jump. And what's with the fucking EXCLAMATION marks?
>>>> It read like you were bursting into hysterical shrill laughter at your
>>>> own non-jokes every four seconds – as if Joe Pasquale suddenly developed
>>>> paranoid schizophrenia. At the end of it I wanted you to go and have a
>>>> long lie down in a floatation tank made of lead and dumped at sea.

>>>>> From : Nicola Murray [mailto : nicolamurray@dosac.gov.uk]
>>>>> To : Malcolm Tucker [mailto : mtucker@gov.org.uk]
>>>>> Subject : Re : Re : Re : Re : Re : Press

>>>>> OK! Constructive criticism! Thanks!!!

>>>>>> **From :** Malcolm Tucker [mailto : mtucker@gov.org.uk]
>>>>>> **To :** Nicola Murray [mailto : nicolamurray@dosac.gov.uk]
>>>>>> **Subject : Re : Re : Re : Re : Re : Re : Press**

>>>>>> Oh! Ironic use of exclamation marks! Very fucking funny! I bet
>>>>>> you wish you'd been born Spanish so you could use twice as many
>>>>>> of the fuckers. I'll be popping in for a chat about this debacle soon.
>>>>>> In the mean time, I would like to reiterate FOR THE FOURTH
>>>>>> TIME that I think you should get therapy. Granted, I was joking to
>>>>>> begin with. BUT I'm not joking any more!!!!! Or am I?

>>>>>> NO I'M FUCKING NOT!!!
>>>>>> !!!!!!!!!!!!!!!!!!!!!!!!!!!!!!!!!

Waitrose

Employee Self-Assessment Form (D1H2)

YOU

Name:

Terri Thelma Elizabeth Coverley

Current position:

Deputy Head of Press. For Waitrose, obviously (!!)

Years in current position:

Two years (2)

Please attach a recent photograph:

I have done this (see attached photo)

YOUR JOB

What, in your opinion, is the most important activity you perform?

In my opinion the most important activity I perform is basically all of them. It's a very stressful job!! Not that I'm complaining! (Although I did make a formal complaint about hours in May.)

Which of your job tasks provides you with the greatest professional satisfaction?

The job task(s) that provide(s?) me with the greatest professional satisfaction is, again, basically, all of them. I love my job! Even the stressful parts and the evenings where sometimes I might have to stay later than expected and miss my wine club. (This has happened four times.)

What do you feel are your strengths?

My strengths are that I get on with the job in hand efficiently and without complaint, even if I actually have a perfect right to complain about some particular aspect or aspects of it.
I am positive and professional in everything I do and can take criticism on the chin even when it is obviously nonsense.
I am a self-starter but also a team player who is comfortable working by myself, or in a team.

What do you feel are your weaknesses?

Cheeky!

YOUR GOALS

What work-related goals have you set for yourself?

The goals I have set myself are to be better at my job and to maybe get home a bit earlier.

Where do you see yourself in five years' time?

Hopefuly working in the Civil Service! I'm joking - I see myself here, being better at my job, obviously, hopefully promoted with better money and holiday entitlement and more flexible hours, just self-starting and team-playing like a good 'un!!

CONFIDENTIAL
To be filled in by employee's immediate superior or line manager

Overall competence (out of 10) 3

Attitude to work (out of 10) 2

Judgement (out of 10) 4

Interpersonal skills (out of 10) 2

Openness to organisational change (out of 10) 2

From : Ollie [mailto : olliereeder@dosac.gov.uk]
To : Malcolm [mailto : mtucker@gov.org.uk]
Subject : **URGENT: Glenn Is The New Stephen Fry**

Malcolm,
Thought you should know that there might be a problem looming.
Glenn Cullen (20th Century blundering Luddite who still hits his
keyboard as if it's a 1949 Olympia typewriter) has joined Twitter
(21st Century social network that spreads gossip faster than
sneezed norovirus). I don't think Glenn gets the crucial difference
between private and public posts. Or the inevitability that people
will find out who "@PULSEFINGER Location: Grapevine Central"
actually is. He's also confused/combined concepts of pissed/off-
piste. He scribbled down his user name and password on a post-it
and stuck it on his monitor. I've pasted his timeline below.

Best, Ollie.

pulsefinger

HAIKU OF THE DAY: Nicola Murray/
Emptiness shrouded in fear/Silly
fucking cow. [thanks, Ben!]
less than a minute ago via web

PERSONAL: Senior political adviser to Cabinet
member, GSOH, non–smoker, late 40s, rugged,
fun, WLTM lady 25–40 for 'who knows?'. 'DM'
me!
45 minutes ago via web

Some insider smells: Prince of Wales (lavender
and spearmint). Kay Burley (pear drops). Rod
Liddle (rabbit hutch).
9:15 AM Jun 17th via web

DM: John, I want to tell that cocaine anecdote.
Can you set up a twitterfeed whatnot so it just
goes to people who don't know Suzy? Cheers.
1:45 PM Jun 16th via web

Name pulsefinger
Location Grapevine
Central
Bio In The Know (and fun
to know!)

44	23	6
following	followers	listed

Tweets 19

Favorites

Following View all...

RSS feed of
PULSEFINGER's tweets RSS
feed of PULSEFINGER's
favorites

Planning authorities: read small print in new White Paper if you don't want a huge fucking detention centre on nearest bit of Green Belt.

9:03 AM Jun 16th via web

FACT: a certain 30-something special adviser at DoSAC was NOT on a fact-finder to Belfast last week, he was getting his end away with a cert.

11:34 AM Jun 15th via web

Seen leaving Portcullis House with a Tesco bag full of suspiciously 'clinking' cargo: a certain PPS who is always 'just being sociable'!!!

4:12 PM Jun 12th via web

Ha ha we're all calling Treasury Frank's new boyfriend 'Black Rod' NB this is not racist as he is black though NB his name is not Rod. [?]

10:09 AM Jun 11th via web

Hey, 'Twitterverse'! Anyone know of a good literary agent? I'm a senior political adviser to a Cabinet member and have a story to kiss/tell.

3:39 PM Jun 9th via web

Politicians today aren't a fucking patch on those of yesteryear. I once had tea and Bourbons with Harold Wilson. True story. Happy days.

9:52 AM Jun 9th via web

DM: John, how do I get rid of the messages I've sent that I don't want anyone to read? Also, can I actually email [Terri, say] from Twitter?

4:12 PM Jun 5th via web

Which senior Opposition backbencher is now doubly incontinent and requires a cortisone injection before every TV appearance? I KNOW...

2:23 PM Jun 5th via web

Please ignore my teets today, am 1 senior adviser to Cabinet member 2 bit jet lagged 3 accidentally pissed because of drink/time zone diff!

7:23 AM Jun 3rd via web

@TelegraphBlogs Wd you be interstd in regular dspatchs fm the Wstmnstr coalface? Am senior advisr to Cabinet mmber & cd make thm 'Whiggish'.

7:21 AM Jun 3rd via web in reply to TelegraphBlogs

@BBCRadio4 ...are "Now Libby Purves..." It is very difficult making a coherent argument for the Licence Fee, never mind Jenni Fucking Murray.
7:08 AM Jun 3rd via web in reply to BBCRadio4

@BBCRadio4 I write as a senior political adviser to a Cabinet member, to tell you that the most depressing three words in the fucking world
7:06 AM Jun 3rd via web in reply to BBCRadio4

@IsraelMFA I am a senior political adviser to a member of the Cabinet of the British Government, and I have to say you have fucked up.
6:49 AM Jun 3rd via web in reply to IsraelMFA

As a senior political adviser to a member of Cabinet I can tell you the mood in Westminster this morning is fucking sombre. More later.
6:06 AM Jun 3rd via web

Testing...testing. Will anyone be able to see this message, John?
5:56 PM May 20th via web

From : Malcolm [mailto : mtucker@gov.org.uk]
To : Ollie [mailto : olliereeder@dosac.gov.uk]
Subject: Arsethumb

Thanks for this. I can see you in your wee blazer with the fucking prefect's badge. "Please Miss, Watson did a widdle in the tuck shop sink. Should I tell him to come and see you for detention?" No, seriously, we need to smother this foaming twatabout NOW. I want you to do the following:
• Set up an account as Joanna Lumley. Send fucking@anchovyfinger a little note from her, asking him to get in touch. She's lonely and loves his 'tits' or whatever those little messages are called. Set up a clandestine meeting somewhere soon. I'll be there waiting.
• Then disable his account. Get IT to set up a page that comes up every time he tries to log on, saying Twitter's busy, it's fucking collapsed under the weight of singing fucking penguins on YouTube or whatever you simpering tossers are watching this week.
• Delete everything he's posted.
• Actually, I can't be arsed with the Lumley Manoeuvre. Keep him at his desk. I'm coming over to delete his fucking face with a scaffolding pole. Now.

Memo: Lord Nicholson
To: Malcolm Tucker

Malcolm

Another one of my cross memos to add to your collection (though, strictly speaking, these are embargoed for 30 years, so don't even think about it).

As you know I've been actioned by the PM to implement a radical top-through of all policy points within government. Which means I have the utmost sanction to go anywhere I please, and ask whatever I popping well like.

And I have been rather quietly getting the answers I need, without any threats of violence. Unlike you, I do not wield a knuckleduster or a fanny-hammer or some such. No, Malcolm, my weapon of choice is the good old-fashioned yellow post-it note. I find a simple idea or query, a tasty suggestion or a pithy summary of the central concerns, written on a bog standard post-it and immediately whooshed to the relevant desk, can furnish me with a solution far faster than any of your weapons of crass obstruction. I call them my 'snowflakes' but I believe they're known round Whitehall as Julius' Yellow Peril.

Now, a small birdy spoke to me at Glyndebourne the other day (Rameau, taken rather too briskly by Sir Simon the aptly-named Rattle) and he told me you've been collecting these Snowflakes for your own private amusement and no-doubt future publication in a salacious Diary. Can I remind you that the post-its are Crown Property and therefore not to be brandished in front of your publishers like a trayful of appetising Mr Kiplings?

Joking aside, I'm really rather cross about this and I can tell you now, if the stickies are not returned pronto I may have to take the matter internally.

Yours, Lord Nicholson

WHY ARE THERE NO MAGISTRATES IN NEWPORT?

CAN WE HAVE A BOMB AUDIT?

I SEEM TO HAVE 7 REPORTS FROM ONLY 5 INQUIRIES. WHAT THE HELL'S GOING ON? (AND NO, I'M NOT LAUNCHING ANOTHER INQUIRY).

20/20 CRICKET: WHY NOT 20/20 QUESTION TIME? I'M SERIOUS. MAKE SURE THE P.M. SEES THIS.

I WANT A FAN OF ACTION POINTS ON IMMIGRATION

COULD WE PLEASE CUT DOWN ON STATE FUNERALS!!

WHAT THE BLEEDIN' HELL ARE 'APPS'?

HEALTH DEPT. STAIRS. FROM NOW ON, WALK UP STAIRS BY MOORS ST. ENTRANCE, AND DOWN NEXT TO COULSTON SQUARE. THERE'S TOO MUCH DISRUPTIVE BANTER WHEN GROUPS COLLIDE.

WHY DO I NOT LIKE THE IDEA OF WIND FARMS NEXT TO CREMATORIA?

HAS ANYONE DONE A CORRELATION BETWEEN REGIONAL SENTENCING PATTERNS AND JUDGES' DIETS? THROWS UP SOME INTERESTING ANOMALIES

BEACONS OF EXCELLENCE
TORCHES OF RESPECT?
ROCKETS OF EXPERIENCE?
MISSILES OF UNDERSTANDING?

WE TALK OF INNER-CITY AND OUTER CITY. WE FORGET THE PEOPLE WHO LIVE IN BETWEEN. READ MY DEMOS SPEECH ON 'THE CITY SANDWICH'.

STOP THE BISHOP OF SOUTHWARK USING TWITTER

CRIME CLUSTER?
DELINQUENCY POINTS?
NODES OF LAWLESSNESS?

I THINK DUAL PURPOSE PROCUREMENT HAS GOT LEGS

LANDFILL SITES? WHY NOT 'SCULPTED DEPOSIT CENTRES'?

THERE'S A PRIZE FOR WHICH PART OF THE HOME OFFICE CAN GET THEIR CRIME STATS OUT QUICKEST. BIT OF FUN!

CAN YOU GIVE JEREMY A KICKING FROM ME OVER THE STAFFORDSHIRE PRISON BREAK-OUT?

MULTI-STOREY FORESTS?

To: Donald Feathermill
From: Ben Swain

Greetings Donaldo, la Donna me mobile, the Donster, etc.

In a bit of a rush, so leaving it to you to spank this one out for me.

I'm thinking of putting together a book to come out same time as my leadership bid. Haven't had time to get the final manushit together, so thought you might be able to take the beef of some of my speeches and cobble a worthy tome out of it. I'm looking for something that captures the authentic Ben Swain voice, while maybe get a bit of Nick Hornby in there too.

Here's a thick clod of some transcripts of spontaneous remarks I've been making up and down North London at leadership junkets this past month. They're what I call my Think Thoughts, which may well be the title of the book, although I'm also toying with 'Britain: It Ain't Broken'.

I think you'll see the Think Thoughts add up to a compelling argument for a successful leadership bid, or they will once you sort out the syntax and bung in the relevant figures.

Could you process this all by next Wednesday and then send to Faber? There's a guy there on standby. Called Stephen, I think. Use Google if not sure.

If there's anything that needs clarification, don't hesitate to ring my assistant Amanda.

So, get to it. If this leadership thing comes off, I guarantee you a step up in office furnishings. More power to your elbow, me ol' mucker. Quietly flows the Don, eh?

Ben

PS C U @ Hay-on-Wye !

 dosac

This is a transcript of what I said. It needs cohering a bit. I was tired and anyway had to stand in for Nicola Murray at short notice since she had 'care issues' apparently.   B.

I believe in communities for the very simple reason I was fortunate to come from a happy one, and I believe that's the case for most people in the wider sector.

But how often do we forget that Communities is also a state of mind as well as an Estate of Houses? ie, that sense of connectedness that gives someone, Me, a sense of true purpose when I can help another someone, You or Your Parents or Cousins? It's the impulse within us to want to do something for others, to reach out beyond our own living room, kitchenette or whatever, a boat-house in some cases, I visited one yesterday and was impressed with what you could fit in it, and actually participate in a wider family of skills (for example, my brother is a great football player, and when we were younger he always used to help run some junior teams at the local youth club. I have a terrible left ankle which was always a regret so I never played, but I always helped out afterwards).

So you see that here Communities becomes a doing word in a sense. I see it like one of those lighthouses that send out a beam of light to guide you round treacherous rocks girdling a shore. But with the one difference, in that it's not warning you off, but drawing you in. Communities says to the ordinary citizen, 'Come here, Look at me, What d'you think?' And then, 'Stay, please. I need help'.

That's what my personal credo is in a nutshell; how we can utilise all the complexities of state-supported organisations and incentives and interlace them with the private-sector lines of action and personal paths of opportunity to create what I call a Fretwork of Action.

BRITAIN ABROAD

This for me is the lifeblood of what I believe, which is, What is Britain's place in the wider world? I mean by this, not just Europe, not just the U.S. (though that is crucially important, perhaps the most important relationship bar none) but, of course, Africa. And there is also India and China to think about. So there, you see, the world is a lot different to how it looked even ten years ago, and that's the factor we've going to have to grapple with if we've not to be left behind. I want to state here and now my overwhelming opposition to the Euro.

Don, leave this untouched. I'm proud of this one. Though if you could add a couple of lines at the end to take it up to the Obamasphere, then two Proms tickets could be yours. B x

People say, oh God, we've got a recession. I say, wait, wait, what we have is, yes, awful, and certainly for a lot of people, but it's also an opportunity. For if we can invest once more in those old-fashioned core industries like manufacturing and useful equipment and white goods, then can we not re-energise the economy for the future?

What I'm saying is, How many people does it take to make a fridge? I've been to Coventry, and it's seven. But if we're building not just fridges but also toasters, i-Pod docks, heaters, tractor-parts, cookers, sandwich makers, electronic whisking machines, standard lamps, then there's no end to what we can achieve.

And I'd happily argue twelve minutes with Paxman to say they're vital to getting Britain moving.

Appraisal Form

Line Manager's Annual Performance Review

Form A/CG 12a

To be completed annually for each Grade IIIV (ia) P-T staff member by their RS-3 superior.

Completed by: Terri Coverley
Regarding: Robyn Murdoch

Punctuality:

Occasional. And then it's like we should be impressed. As in, 'Look Terri! Look who's in at nine?!' - oh right, everyone. And you. For once!

Attitude:

Swings wildly between irritatingly eager to please and long periods of surly petulance.

Skillset:

Robyn is able to type up a simple press release given heavy guidance and continual encouragement.

Recommendation for advancement:

It may be that like an odd little frog in a David Attenborough rainforest documentary Robyn has become adapted to life in the tropical pond that is the DOSAC private office. I do not believe she would thrive elsewhere!

From : Terri [mailto : terricoverley@dosac.gov.uk]
To : John [mailto : johnlopard@dosac.gov.uk]
Subject: **Annual reviews**

John
You know the annual performance review forms that we now have to do, they are confidential aren't they?

Cheers
Tezza

From : John [mailto : johnlopard@dosac.gov.uk]
To : Terri [mailto : terricoverley@dosac.gov.uk]
Subject: Re : **Annual reviews**

Dear Ms Coverley

Regarding your recent inquiry. Assessment information is of course totally confidential.
Although obviously in the case of a freedom of information request or industrial tribunal
the employee in question would naturally have access to all their assessments.

Yours

John Lopard
Head of Personnel
Department of Social Affairs and Citizenship

Appraisal Form

Line Manager's Annual Performance Review   Form A/CG 12a

To be completed annually for each Grade IIIV (ia) P-T staff member by their
RS-3 superior.

Completed by: `Terri Coverley`

Regarding: `Robyn Murdoch`

Punctuality:

`Acceptable.`

Attitude:

`Acceptable.`

Skillset:

`Acceptable.`

Recommendation for adva

`Acceptable.`

From : Terri [mailto : terricoverley@dosac.gov.uk]
To : John [mailto : johnlopard@dosac.gov.uk]
Subject: Re : Re : **Annual reviews**

Dear Mr Lopard

It appears that some 'office joker' has had access to my
log-in information and in a humorous way which I do not
intend to pursue as a breach of security, filled in some
staff assessments in a comical fashion. Can you therefore
burn and delete the 'pretend' appraisal of Robyn Murdoch
recently sent through and also the one for Hugh Kitchener
containing the phrase, 'more mince than Tescos'. The
correct versions are attached.

Yours Sincerely

Terri Coverley
Senior Press Officer DOSAC

STAFF

PETER
MANNION

STAFF NO: 84788
DEPT. NO: COMM3
SEC CODE: A

6 98458 84788 1

CABINET OFFICE
STAFF

STEVEN FLEMING

STAFF NO: 86277
DEPT. NO: COMM2
SEC CODE: A

6 98458 86277 8

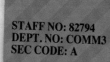

STAFF

PHILIP
SMITH

STAFF NO: 82794
DEPT. NO: COMM3
SEC CODE: A

6 98458 82794 4

STAFF

EMMA
MESSINGER

STAFF NO: 84317
DEPT. NO: COMM3
SEC CODE: A

6 98458 84317 3

CABINET OFFICE
STAFF

JULIUS
NICHOLSON

STAFF NO: 85433
DEPT. NO: COMM2
SEC CODE: A

6 98458 85433 9

STAFF

STEWART
PEARSON

STAFF NO: 85178
DEPT. NO: COMM3
SEC CODE: A

6 98458 85178 9

Mannion

From : Malcolm Tucker [mailto: dontblamemenowthateverythingisfucked@gmail.com]
To : Ollie Reeder [mailto: olliereeder63@parliament.co.uk]
Subject : Pull your thumb out of your arse and stick a fucking Roman Candle up there

Good Morning you Worthless Human Pop Tart.

Where are the Mannion attack points?

I seem to recall I requested these before the fucking election – and if a week is a long time in politics that means I asked about … oh A MILLION YEARS AGO.

I realise you're probably busy slapping on the Paco Rabanne and making your CV look like it's wearing a Wonderbra but don't even think about taking that further pal. If I hear you've put the feelers out I will punch your cock so far inside your body you'll need more sex tests than Caster Semenya.

Now get on the fucking case you lanky streak of dysentery.

I expect a reply before you've finished reading this. And before I've finished typing it. So where is it fuck stain?

M

> From : Ollie Reeder [mailto: olliereeder63@parliament.co.uk]
> To : Malcolm Tucker [mailto:dontblamemenowthateverythingisfucked
> @gmail.com]
> Subject : All The Bad Things Peter Mannion Has Ever Thought and Done
> [File attached : Peter Mannion Attack Points Strategy Document.doc]

> Hi Malc,

> Thanks for your lovely email. Sorry not to get back sooner – been
> slightly busy here mopping up the aftermath of you shooting the party
> in the foot and head and anus.

> Also thought you might be a bit busy contemplating the electoral
> wilderness and deciding what the point of you is now. Heard you're
> thinking about kayaking round Scandinavia for people with no lymph
> nodes. Any truth to that? Or are you sticking with co-ordinating the
> world's biggest oatcake for National Literacy Day?

> Here are the Mannion bullet points you requested.

> Apologies they're not quite as finessed as I'd hoped but as I say been
> distracted by the carnage, counting the casualties, patching up the
> wounded, wondering where/ who our leader is, trying to find an office,
> procuring new letter-headed paper, etc, etc, yada yada, blah blah, la
> la la.

> Ollie

Peter Mannion
Attack Points

Okay. Here's the obvious stuff I could crib straight from Wikipedia.

(Left) Mannion and his wife and (right) here's his bit of fluff getting doorstepped

Love child

Famously fathered a love child in 1989 with his then mistress, Jackie Williamson, who was at the time an opposition MP. (Saucy!) Private Eye did a whole thing about him looking like Robert Palmer and being 'Addicted to Love (Children)'. Plus various other jokes about cross-party alliances and the sordid sex practice of 'back-benching'. Mannion tried to deal with it by being funny – at one point answering the door to the press while playing Love Shack by The B-52s loudly on his stereo. He later went on Have I Got News For You and was generally regarded to have been 'not totally unfunny'. Except by Mrs. Mannion.

Choice quotes from the time :

'Our eyes met during a late night sitting on EEC fishery reform. The atmosphere was electric. In the bar afterwards he asked me about the cap and said, "I'm not talking about our Common Agricultural Policy". It sounds cheesy now but the way he said it was unbelievably sexy and I did go a bit moist'. Jackie Williamson.

'He's a massive, massive bastard'. Sally Mannion.

'Public embarrassment is actually very liberating. You stop caring about what people think. I could do anything now – I could take a dump on a dwarf, who cares? Not me. Alright, maybe the dwarf'. Peter Mannion.

Drink-driving

On his way home from a CBI bash in the City Mannion crashed his car into a woman's garden. A startled Mrs. McLaughlin awoke to find Mannion 'on his hands and knees in the middle of my roses laughing like an idiot'. 'It wasn't funny', she added. Mannion said : 'I swerved to avoid killing a baby hedgehog because I thought it might puncture my tyres'. He later said, 'I look forward to appearing on the front cover of Private Eye again. It would appear I am to Private Eye what Cindy Crawford is to Vogue'.

Drink-driving

On holiday in 1993 he drunkenly ran his yacht into another yacht off the coast of Ithaca. Said, 'the ocean made a sudden unexpected up and down motion' that threw him off course.

'Sexting' accusation

Two years ago Mannion sent a 'sexy' text message to a work experience kid. Claimed it was meant for his wife. To be fair, it probably was meant for his wife. He's not exactly an Early Adopter. He's only just chucked his Sony Walkman. The sexy message also wasn't that sexy. 'Get your knickers off! I'm pissed!'

Mass murderer

On the board of not one but three major tobacco firms currently deliberately trying to kill children in Africa and Asia. Although, to be fair, does smoke himself – so he's no hypocrite.

So. That's the obvious stuff. What else can we use against him? Blue sky thinking …

Has floppy hair

Could be a wig. Possibly made by children in a sweatshop in Honduras. Possibly made out of hair stolen from the rotting corpse of Robert Palmer.

Looks like Robert Palmer

He looks like Robert Palmer.

He's a bit dim

He only got a third class degree from Cambridge.
For shame. And it was in Art History. For shame.

Fancy dress faux pas

Once went to a fancy dress party at University dressed
as an aborted foetus. Allegedly.

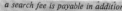

a search fee is payable in addition.

Registra		
1 862. Birth in the Sub-distr		
Columns :—	1	2
No.	When and where born	Name, if any

He's old

He's like 62 or some shit FFS. We've got to be
able to do something with that.

He takes Viagra

Maybe he takes Viagra?

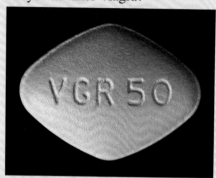

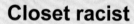

Sick sense of humour

Behind closed doors he likes to laugh
about the 1,198 innocent lives lost on the
Lusitania. Once said, 'Wouldn't it have
been funny if Princess Diana had driven
into the Twin Towers and everyone had
died that way? Including Jade Goody who
happened to be failing to complete the New
York marathon at the time.' What a bastard.

Bizarre fantasies

Likes to fantasise about blowing up zeppelins
full of kittens using a machine gun that is
actually his penis. Bit odd?

Closet racist

Well known for his love of
Robinsons' jam. Once in a game of
Scrabble used the word 'jiggerboos'.
Admittedly, not a bad score but is
that any kind of defence?

Weirdly superstitious

Refuses to look at policy ideas if there's a
magpie on his desk. Won't do any work until a
young woman tugs him off while saying, 'Hello
Mr. Magpie where's your wife today?' to which
he has to reply, 'Who gives a fuck, I'm getting a
lovely hand shandy'.

From : Malcolm Tucker [mailto: dontblamemenowthateverythingisfucked@
gmail.com]
To : Peter Mannion [mailto: petermannion@tory.org]
CC : Ollie Reeder [mailto: olliereeder63@parliament.co.uk]
Subject : Your Sordid Past

Hi Peter,

Asked Ollie Reeder if could come up with some attack points on you. Thought
you might like to see what he'd come up with. Think you might find it amusing.

Although, on a serious note, it's so piss-poor I wondered if I could ask if you
could add to it?

Any help greatly appreciated. This is what I've got to work with these days.

Best,
Malcolm

> From : Peter Mannion [mailto: petermannion@tory.org]
> To : Malcolm Tucker [mailto: dontblamemenowthateverythingisfucked@
> gmail.com]
> CC : Ollie Reeder [mailto: olliereeder63@parliament.co.uk]
> Subject : My Sordid Past
>
> Malcolm,
>
> It's coming to something when you have to help the Opposition come up with
> ways to attack you. But since Punch and Judy politics are now firmly a thing of
> the past I suppose I should reach out across the party divide and help you out.
>
> You may want to use some/ all of the following …
>
> Friends with Fred 'The Shred' Goodwin.
>
> Once sat next to Abu Hamza at a dinner party and helped shell his pistachios.
> (That's not a euphemism.)
>
> Was overheard at Party Conference in '94 describing his then Prime Minister
> as 'about as exciting as Chlamydia'.
>
> Got annoyed by someone eating smelly food on the tube so farted in their face.
>
> Once spent ten grand on a bottle of wine at a drunken lunch with City bankers.
> Didn't bother to finish it because it tasted a bit five grand-y.
>
> Not a real MP. Actually an imposter.
>
> Got drunk with Black Rod and took a slash on the Queen's tiara. (Again, not a
> euphemism.)

Once pushed a younger, more idealistic MP to his death from top of St. Stephen's Tower.

Hope that helps!

All the best,

Peter

Dictated but not read as still concerned email might be the work of the Devil.

****

From : Ollie Reeder [mailto: olliereeder63@parliament.co.uk]
To : Malcolm Tucker [mailto: dontblamemenowthateverythingisfucked@gmail.com]
Subject : You evil bastard

For fuck's sake Malcolm. What the fuck?! Have you fucking lost it?

> From : Malcolm Tucker [mailto:
> dontblamemenowthateverythingisfucked@gmail.com]
> To : Ollie Reeder [mailto: olliereeder63@parliament.co.uk]
> Subject : RE : You evil bastard

> Ancient Chinese proverb : Who am I? Uncle Cunt?

>> From : Ollie Reeder [mailto: olliereeder63@parliament.co.uk]
>> To : Malcolm Tucker [mailto:
>> dontblamemenowthateverythingisfucked@gmail.com]
>> Subject : RE : RE : You evil bastard

>> What the fuck is that supposed to mean?

>>> From : Malcolm Tucker [mailto:
>>> dontblamemenowthateverythingisfucked@gmail.com]
>>> To : Ollie Reeder [mailto: olliereeder63@parliament.co.uk]
>>> Subject : RE : RE : RE : You evil bastard

>>> Ancient Iranian proverb : I think you know what it means.
>>>
>>> Ancient Greek proverb : Don't start a cock fight unless
>>> you're prepared to be fucked up the arse so hard you puke
>>> your own thorax.

>>> Contemporary British proverb : Now do some fucking
>>> work.

Churchill College Tolkien Society
CHURCHILL COLLEGE, CAMBRIDGE
President: Philip Smith Treasurer: Philip Smith

"I do not love the bright sword for its sharpness, nor the arrow for its swiftness, nor the warrior for his glory. I love only that which they defend."

My planned trajectory, by Philip Smith
Michaelmas Term, 1990
My room (8A), Cantab

UPDATED, MARCH 2009. COSTA COFFEE, BROMLEY.

1991
**Become head of the University
Libertarian Society.**

Kate Nichols got the ULs. I wonder why? Is it because she was the most able candidate with an unrivalled and precocious knowledge of Free Market Economics which even Robert Robinson commented on when we all appeared on "Ask The Family" in 1982? Or is it because she was blonde and pretty and everyone (except me) fancied her?

1992
Graduate with a starred first in PPS.

Had the runs for the History of Political Thought paper and asked them to take this into account, as I had to leave the hall 8 times, and each time an invigilator had to come with me and remain in the toilet, which meant I couldn't poo. And the night before Comparative Politics paper Kate Nichols accused me of touching her inappropriately in the Buttery and said she would lodge a complaint, so my mind was elsewhere. Given all that, a 2:2 was bloody good going.

1994
**Get awarded the Kennedy Scholarship
at Harvard, leading to an internship
in Washington.**

It's who you know.

1998
**Marry Kelly LeBrock from 'Weird
Science'.**

Wasn't in America so this didn't happen.
Quite glad, she aged badly.

```
2002
MP for safe constituency (Dorking?
Witney?)
```

Didn't get on the list because I wasn't "fully chiming with the new direction of the party." More like I wasn't "fully wanking off Tony Cochrane at Dorset Square like Martin was."

```
2003
Start assembling my 'team'. Need a
brainy one (my lieutenant, possibly
future Chancellor to my PM) a funny
one (human, for PR purposes) a
woman (box ticking) someone from a
minority ethnic group (ditto).
```

In retrospect, this was too much like trying to replicate the Double Deckers.

```
2006
Bid for leadership. Make a big deal
of my youth and, without getting
big-headed, my looks. But also my
experience, as I will be 35, which
is the same age Roger Moore was when
he first played Simon Templar in The
Saint. And only an idiot would say
he wasn't a grown-up in that.
```

Not being MP obviously scuppered this. Although this was the year I first became an advisor to Peter Mannion, and I think my youth, looks and experience all played a part in his choosing me for the job. Plus he knows Dad.

```
2011
I will be Prime Minister of the
United Kingdom of Great Britain and
Northern Ireland, First Lord of the
Treasury. The youngest, I predict,
since 1812. I will have achieved
a massive landslide, having taken
the British people with me in the
greatest populist movement since
Mussolini's March on Rome in 1922.
```

Still a year to go!

From : Phillip.Smith@gmail
To : SallyMannion1@btinternet.com
Subject : New policy angle?

Hello Sally

Can you print this off for Peter? I know he never looks at his email.
Peter. I was reading the New Scientist and an article in there suggested to me that
a relatively small set of public health policies could make a significant difference
to the life expectancies of the population. I wondered if: '10 steps to make the
nation live 10 years more' might not be a good policy angle? Let me know your
thoughts.

Yours, as ever, with regards, and best wishes etc

Philip

From : OllieReeder@hotpotatoes.com
To : Nmurray@btinternet.com
Subject : Good new policy?

Nicola

After your late night rant/motivational chat last night about the
'vacuity and shit-ness' of modern political thinking and in particular,
me, I went home and had a rummage around my home computers
and the selection of challenging/mould-breaking ideas therein and
came up with the below:

I was reading the New Scientist and an article in there suggested to
me that a relatively small set of public health policies could make
a significant difference to the life expectancies of the population. I
wondered if : '10 steps to make the nation live 10 years more might
not be a good policy angle'? Let me know your thoughts?

Interesting?

Word out.

Ollie

Finally Ollie, YES!
Let's go with this. BIG TIME!
I like this! I LOVE THIS!!

It's so 'me'. In fact, did I mention something like
this to you on the train to Leamington once?
This sounds so like me, I wondered if it
was me?
But no matter, the main thing is I think
you/I have really got something here!

It's simple. It's direct. It's full of joy de vivre,
optimism, hope, it's sexy and not necessarily
too expensive!

I want all hands to the pump, a list
of ten policy proposals that might add up
to a gain in 10 years life expectancy.

Ollie, well done. And please don't take my comments on Wednesday evening to heart. You were tired. It's worth saying for the record that I like your face. I think you have a good sense of personal style.

I think you have brains for brains, not whatever I might have suggested in the heat of the moment.

And I most definitely would not wish to suggest you had either a small male organ of procreation or lacked entirely the organs of sperm production.

Onwards and upwards my friend!

Nicky
            xxx

From: Nicola Murray
To: Malcolm Tucker

Malcolm

We have been blue-skying a policy pitch under the heading '10 steps for 10 more years'. I'm very excited. The below are our 10 points (actually 6 but we wondered if people would get bored after the first 6? Maybe the others could be fillers, or even a nice way to slip in some banking/capital gains reforms?)

Anyway, see what you think. If you're agreeable I think this could be something that one day (and I blush as I write this) might stand next to the Beveridge Report and the founding of the NHS as a significant moment in our political history. (I can't believe I wrote that, but I do believe I really did!)

Let me know ASAP if you think it needs any tweaks and we can talk about the logistics of the PM and I launching this together?

Regards

Nicola

Nicola Murray

Secretary of State for Social Affairs and Citizenship
(but soon possibly moving upwards and onwards!!!??)

10 for 10 Policy Proposals

- **Total ban on TV advertising of all processed foods with fat & sugar content above that recommended by the World Health Organisation.**

  THIS MAYBE THE SINGLE MOST UNWORKABLE POLICY IDEA I HAVE EVER COME ACROSS. WELL DONE. COLLECT YOUR PLUTONIUM ENRICHED MEDAL FROM ME AFTER SCHOOL.

- **One nutritionally balanced organically sourced fresh cooked meal provided free to all school children.**

  IS IT PRETTY IN YOUR DREAM WORLD NICOLA? I'D LIKE TO TAKE LSD AND COME THERE WITH YOU ONE DAY.

- **Total ban on alcohol sponsorship and TV and print advertising.**

  SORRY — I SPOKE TOO SOON. THIS IS THE MOST UNWORKABLE POLICY IDEA I HAVE EVER SEEN.

- **Compel private health clubs to offer membership to recipients of tax credits referred for one-on-one personal training by their doctors**

  WHO DO YOU THINK YOU'RE KIDDING MRS. STALIN? YOU MAY WANT AN 18 STONE SCAFFOLDER SPRAYING YOU WITH CHAV JUICE DOWN CHAMPNEYS — I DO NOT. NOR DOES THE GREAT BRITISH PUBLIC.

- **Free entry to all leisure centres and sport facilities for under 16s.**

  GREAT! HOW ARE YOU GOING TO PAY FOR THIS ONE? MAKE THE CHANGING ROOMS SEE-THROUGH AND CHARGE THE PERVS TO COME AND WATCH?

- **To be paid for by a super-tax on nutritionally useless carbonated drinks.**

  OH NO, YOU'VE THOUGHT OF AN EVEN LESS POLITICALLY SALEABLE IDEA — CONGRATULATIONS. HAVE A COKE AND A SURCHARGE. "I'D LIKE TO TEACH THE WORLD TO SING, MURRAY'S A FUCKHEAD, IN PERFECT HARMONY."

From: Nicola@Home [mailto : Nmurray@btinternet.com]
To: Glenn Cullen [mailto : GlennyC@aol.com]
Subject : **NHM!!**

4.03AM

Glenn

Okay, I've been up all night and I really think that even if the policy is going to have to work within certain political and financial constraints we can really play this one big. I don't like the term relaunch but I think this is something which could boost my profile in a way that will be useful to the party and yes, eventually, to the nation.

I'm not going to be falsely modest with you Glenn, I think I can trust you, and I do think the party will be looking for a new leader in the next eighteen months and I'm not ashamed to say I entered politics in order to do things and the best way to do things is to actually do them and if that involves being Foreign Secretary or Prime Minister then, so be it, I do not seek the job, merely the power and prestige that the job accidentally involves.

Anyway, I think for the launch of the 10 for 10 policy – (now re-named the New Health Manifesto (NHM)) we should give it both weight and pizzazz. Here's a vision:

The FA Cup Final, or Olympics. Before the kick off - I sit/stand with David Beckham, Andy Murray, maybe a welsh man and not Tiger Woods, but someone else - and together we launch a campaign to change the way we think about health and longevity in this country (poss globally? Why not!) forever. There are fireworks. There is considerable pizzazz. But at the centre of it is a set of very simple very direct very thorough policy proposals and government initiatives which we will work out next week (NB, not the old ones) which will establish this department and also me as a heavyweight of politics.

Quite a dream isn't it?

Glenn, can you talk to Terri and Ollie and as they say on Star Trek, make it so!

Nicola.

Glenn—
Thanks for leaving this
print out for me. It's been
a hard day. feel like I've
been trying to shit an
Easter Island head and
get it on Newsnight
talking sense.

This gave me a right
larf. I owe you a print
Mac

Murray: 'Pain in the bum'

Keiran Cox: British No. 6

COX OUT

BRITISH NUMBER 6 seed Kieran Cox appeared at a photo call with gaffe-prone Minister Nicola Murray yesterday. But it looks like he's going to be out of the picture even quicker than bumbling Murray after losing out to Slovenian first-timer Milos Vrancic in straight sets.

Before the first round Stella Artois Tournament tie Nicola Murray said she thought that children might benefit from occasionally eating an additional piece of fruit. But she added she didn't wish to be 'a pain in the bum' about it.

---

dosac

Nicola,

Look. I've been stewing on this but it is just not true to say that the New Health Manifesto (NHM) launch event got 'fuck all coverage'. It's not a very nice thing to say and it quite frankly isn't a fair reflection on all the hard work me and the rest of the team put in. (Voigner is my favourite white grape variety and I missed the tasting on Thursday, so I hope that shows in some way my very real level of commitment). Attached one of the two pieces that made it to print. The other one wasn't very complimentary. But the buzz after the event was excellent. And a man from Wandsworth council is meant to be following up about ordering 30 or more of the 70,000 NHM leaflets. So. Pats on back time methinks!

Terri

RESIGNATION TEMPLATES

Sam:
I've updated the three resignation templates for use when purging ministers. As before, I've suggested an outline for the P.M.'s measured response to each of the three scenarios. Do me a favour — once it's been printed, can you leave copies out for Nicola Murray to leaf through next time she comes over? We need to keep the dozy fucking cow focused/paranoid. M

EXCHANGE A

Something roughly along these lines when the minister in question has done us a favour by resigning before whatever pressurised calamity we've been holding shut suddenly bursts all over Sky News like some fucking Sony Bravia ad but with explosions of uniformly-coloured shit instead of a paint rainbow. Assume we appreciate them falling on their sword. One good turn deserves another, etc.

From Minister A to PM

Dear Tom,

When we met yesterday you asked me to reconsider my decision to leave the Cabinet. I promised I would defer my final decision until this afternoon. After much soul-searching I have decided with regret and sadness to tender my resignation.

To have served with this Government has been the proudest achievement of my life. To have worked for a Prime Minister whom I regard as the most successful of my lifetime has been an honour. To have counted you as a friend as well as a colleague has been a joy, and a blessing.

As I said yesterday, I believe the sustained campaign against me by certain elements in the media is a distraction the Department does not need at this time, when valuable work remains to be done. I owe it to you, the Government, my constituents and my family to do the right thing by stepping aside now.

Yours,

A

From the PM to Minister A

Dear A,

Yesterday I offered my support to you for whatever course of action you felt was right. I must now honour that commitment and, with the utmost reluctance, accept your resignation.

You have been a loyal colleague and an outstanding minister. I am absolutely convinced that you will return to government in the future. Be assured that you will have my personal backing in the coming weeks.

I know you to be someone of the highest probity and integrity. I very much look forward to working with you again.

Warmest regards to you and [partner's first name],

Tom

EXCHANGE B

To be deployed in the event of Sudden Fuck-Up, when the minister has demonstrated — spectacularly — their extreme fucking uselessness. Assume we do not like Minister B much and owe them nothing. Assume they have been presented with the following career alternatives. One, they dribble out the rest of their political half-life on the back benches before getting hoovered up by a firm of lobbying dronefucks. Two, they take the quick exit from political life via the side door to the car park, where Jamie McDonald is waiting to trundle back and forth over their surprisingly but not infinitely resilient torso in a fucking armoured secret service Mercedes.

From Minister B to PM

Dear Prime Minister,

At our meeting earlier today, I gave you my assurance that I would carefully consider my position as a representative of this Government in the light of what I accept has been a steady and unignorable stream of criticism.

Having reflected, I now wish to tender my resignation. Although I do so with a heavy heart, I fully acknowledge that continuing in my present role would be politically and morally untenable. Throughout my career you and our party colleagues have shown huge support and patience. I accept that under the present circumstances I can no longer expect either with a clear conscience.

It has been a privilege to have worked with some of the finest people I will ever meet. I also wish to make it clear, both in this letter to you and publicly in the days to come, that the decision to resign has been mine and mine alone. And, of course, I also accept sole and full responsibility for any mistakes or errors of judgement that may have occurred.

Yours most sincerely,

B

From the PM to Minister B

Dear B,

Thank you for your letter of resignation, which I accept with some sadness. Although I fully understand the reasons for your departure, I am sure I am not alone in wishing you great success for the future.

You have endured difficult times with great fortitude and self-assurance, and I know you will continue to be a diligent and hard-working constituency MP for as long as you choose to remain in politics.

I have not yet had the opportunity to speak personally to your colleagues at the Department but I am sure they would want to join me in sending you the very best wishes for the future,

Yours,

Tom

EXCHANGE C

Yeah, C For Cunt. Assume that this barrel of piss has decided to tough it out, and has ignored my advice to shit off back to Scorchmark and Queef or wherever their fucking constituency is. Assume that I told them to resign 24 hours ago. Assume that they hid away somewhere, sulkily and pointlessly trying to rally support among Parliamentary party members currently too terrified to even look out of the fucking window. Assume that I have found them, informed them of their resignation, shaken them formally by the throat, told them very fucking enigmatically that they will be putting in much more 'surgery time' in the coming months and tipped off every hack in my bulging contacts book that a PPS had to intervene last week to stop them being arrested, very pissed and racially abusive, at a sex casino in the middle of the fucking afternoon.

From Minister C to PM

Dear Prime Minister,

It is with shame and contrition I offer my resignation. I would like to take this opportunity to apologise to you, to hon. Members of the House and to anyone involved in the recent incident, details of which must remain sub judice pending legal proceedings.

I freely admit that I have let myself down. That is of little consequence when I reflect upon how I have let my colleagues, family and friends down. At this stage I can say very little about the circumstances that now require me to resign with immediate effect.

In due course I hope for healing and forgiveness. For now, Prime Minister, I hope you will allow me to reassure everyone that nobody in the party was privy to the events leading up to my resignation. I will be out of the country until the judicial process requires my presence, seeking time and space to rebuild my life.

Yours,

C [full name]

A Short Public Statement From the Prime Minister

I have today accepted the resignation of C [full name]. A successor will be announced tomorrow morning.

Ref: MT/RTRevised/SC

Friday May 2 1989

The Politics of Dancing

By arts correspondent
Jamie MacDonald

IT IS suddenly fashionable in these times of cross-cultural synergy and symbiosis to proclaim that comedy is the new rock and roll. Well, after a dazzling performance of contemporary dance at Glasgow City Halls by the Canadian company Go Go Boo Boo, I was left wondering if dance might just be the new politics.

Despite a disappointingly small audience for the only appearance by the acclaimed troupe in Scotland this year, it was an electrifying experience. Go Go Boo Boo's work skilfully combines the classical elegance of traditional ballet with a punk sensibility and for THIS inveterate balletomaine at least – dance has been my passion for years - it was an epiphany.

The central piece of the evening was *Reagan In Shades*. It is a powerful and disturbing collage of human movement, live distorted guitar, an endlessly looping tape of a child's voice shrieking out random words, images of oppression projected on to what looks like a gigantic Quaker tapestry, and more. It is utterly immersive, and profoundly moving.

The semi-improvised narrative takes us on an extremely uncomfortable journey into a contemporary political culture of rage and conquest. It is, in short, a parable of America's political-military imperative: to win at any cost and to ignore all moral objections.

The dancers wear business suits, their jerking, pulsing movement reflected in John Lymond's striking set: vertical slabs of shuttered concrete panels moving uncertainly around the stage on a central turntable. As the dancers and the concrete slabs circle and intersect, each becomes a political vector for the other. The visual experience ultimately dissolves into what Gershon calls "instinctive power lines" of mass through space, drained of all "political" meaning.

Summary: wow. I urge you, earnestly, to get to a Go Go Boo Boo gig at the earliest opportunity. A night in their company is exhausting.

Yet exquisite.

Rating: ★★★★★

From : Malc [mailto : mtucker@gov.org.uk]
To : Wee Jamie [mailto : jmacdonald@gov.org.uk]
Subject: Darling, you were exquisite

Hey Jamie, look what I found. You should present this at the next tribunal, show people what a sensitive fucking guy you really are. Honestly mate, I was moved to fucking tears.
M

From : Wee Jamie [mailto : jmacdonald@gov.org.uk]
To : Malc [mailto : mtucker@gov.org.uk]
Subject: CUNT

Fuck you. Fuck you up the Avenue Q. I TOLD you about my Summer of Shame. I remember I spent the whole of July that year trying to get into the arts editor's pants. Penelope. So fucking posh. She could trace her family back to the Norman Fucking Conquest. Unfortunately she never got one in the eye from me. Soon as it was fucking obvious I was going nowhere with Penny I moved from arts to the crime desk. End. Of. Story. OK?

J
Also, I'm pretty sure I didn't even actally GO to this wankfest. Seem to recall cribbing it off some other fucking review.

****

From : Malc [mailto : mtucker@gov.org.uk]
To : Wee Jamie [mailto : jmacdonald@gov.org.uk]
Subject: No No Boo Boo

Nice try, my little snot-nosed nihilist. What would you say if I told you that the person who showed me this cutting ALSO worked at the Glasgow Herald in 1989? And that she remembers you very well? The experimental ponytail? The eyeliner? The blouson? The Sobranie Cocktail? The jazz? M

*

From : Wee Jamie [mailto : jmacdonald@gov.org.uk]
To : Malc [mailto : mtucker@gov.org.uk]
Subject: Re: No No Boo Boo

I would say suck my bollocks you fucking mingetunnel. I have nothing to fucking hide/more to say on this matter. Fuck.

J

Hey Malc

Okay, Paul at the Mirror tipped me off last night that some desperate NHS fuckbag was thinking of trying to sell the PM's medical records to the Mail or Express or the fucking Lancet or something.

Well he isn't any more. Let's just say he's been stopped. Let's just say that. Let's not say how he was stopped. Everyone is better off without that knowledge.

So here they are then - have you seen this shit before? Have you read this catalogue of fucking disintegration? It's like a fucking Burroughs novel. Jesus, the big man has been prescribed to fuck.

Obviously, we all knew Tom had 'issues'. Janet's broken thumb and the wheelie-bin in the pond told us that. But Jesus, looking at this stuff - the guy has necked so many pills, it's like someone let fucking Mama Cass loose in the back of Boots and shouted "Supermarket Sweep!"

Did you know about this? That he was rattling around like a fucking medical piñata?

It's mainly anti-depressants, obviously. There's a sort of potted history of the development of happy pills here - over the years he's had SSRIs, SNRIs, tricyclics, antipsychotics and benzodiazepines. I mean, he should, by rights, be the happiest fucker on the planet by now.

And did you know he was on diet pills in the 90s? And we thought it was the sushi and the low-fat spread and the hepatitis.

Anyway, I suggest you read this stuff, have a big old laugh, show it to Pat and Tony because we owe them from the pub the other night, and then burn the lot. We really don't need the opposition knowing about the medicated soap, and the scalp thing, and the whole arsehole-collapsing-in-Selfridges episode.

Hugs

Jamie

PS. Don't read page 18 while you're eating.

talks of 'dark thoughts' and of having a 'heavy brain'. He says it is like he is 'swimming in thick misery'. When questioned about his 'heavy brain' he says it feels like a 'plumber's toolbag' (NB not a tool belt, which he says is lighter.) Prescribed 40mg Citalopram daily, with a view to *(contd.)*

Form HS/D/129c In confidence

white flakes, some as large as a postage stamp, which fall constantly onto

From : Sam Cassidy – Assistant to Malcolm Tucker [mailto: scassidy@gov.org.uk]
To : Malcolm Tucker
Subject : Oxford offer

You've had an invitation from Professor Andrew Ward to become Oxford University's next Visiting Professor of Communications. It's a twelve month post requiring you to deliver four lectures and attend some dinners. Are you interested?
*

From : Malcolm Tucker [mailto: mtucker@gov.org.uk]
To : Sam Cassidy – Assistant to Malcolm Tucker
Subject : Fuck OFF

For fuckssake. Can't people see I'm busy? I'm working my replacement iron bollocks off here. Get back to them with something like :

Dear Professor Yafflecock,

I have a violent hatred of posh people, arrogant people, academic people, young people and people who live outside of London somewhere that isn't Scotland. I also have a pathological hatred of people who live in Oxford, students, students at Oxford University, professors in general, Professors at Oxford University, people who like rowing, people who like cycling, people who like fucking punts and people who join the Oxford Revue. I saw it once – it was the unfunniest thing I've ever seen and I watch politicians tell jokes for a living. I'd like to have taken a screwdriver to everyone in the Oxford Revue and used it to hack/ chisel/ lever out their funny bones, then used their funny bones to tickle the backs of their throats until they vomited so hard they threw up bits of their own skeleton.

Plus, I'm busy. I'm spending the next twelve months travelling round Britain on a killing spree for charity.

So, probably not.

Sam - can you tidy that up a bit for me?
*

From : Sam Cassidy - Assistant to Malcolm Tucker [mailto: scassidy@gov.org.uk]
To : Andrew Ward
Subject : Extremely generous offer

Dear Professor Ward,

Busy. But thanks! Big fan.

Best wishes,
Malcolm

Sent on behalf of Malcolm Tucker
*

From : Malcolm Tucker [mailto: mtucker@gov.org.uk]
To : Sam Cassidy – Assistant to Malcolm Tucker
Subject : AIDS awareness

Sam,
Can't sleep. Want to send this to Bono.

I've given it some consideration and I'm thinking the best way for you to raise AIDS awareness is to contract it, you bloated yacht-fuck.

M x
*

From : Sam Cassidy – Assistant to Malcolm Tucker [mailto: scassidy@gov.org.uk]
To : Bono
Subject : AIDS awareness

Bono,
Just wanted to say congratulations on the continued work on AIDS awareness. I have an idea for something even more radical. Let's talk soon. It will cost you though – my PA Sam wants four backstage passes to your next London gig.

Best,
Malcolm

Sent on behalf of Malcolm Tucker
*

From : Sam Cassidy – Assistant to Malcolm Tucker [mailto: scassidy@gov.org.uk]
To : Malcolm Tucker
Subject : FW : AIDS awareness

How's this?
S x

From : Malcolm Tucker [mailto: mtucker@gov.org.uk]
To : Sam Cassidy
Subject : RE : AIDS awareness

Funny. But do that again and I will kill you.
M x
*

From : Ed Atkins [mailto: eatkins@gov.org.uk]
To : Malcolm Tucker
Subject : Help!

Dear Malcolm,
We're having a party fundraiser. Wondered if you'd mind contributing an item for auction? A signed photo? A tie you wore on election night? One of your old mobile phones? (You must have quite a collection!) One of the severed heads you keep in your fridge? Haha! Just teasing on that last one. Any help hugely appreciated.

Many thanks in advance,

Ed Atkins
*

From : Malcolm Tucker [mailto: mtucker@gov.org.uk]
To : Sam Cassidy – Assistant to Malcolm Tucker
Subject : No.

My first reaction is to say 'go, fuck yourself pal'. My second reaction is to say the same. My third is to say the same again but with more vehemence/ spittle.
Sam?
*

From : Sam Cassidy – Assistant to Malcolm Tucker [mailto: scassidy@gov.org.uk]
To : Ed Atkins
Subject : FW: RE: Help!

Dear Ed,
I'd love to help. Great cause. I'm sending a football shirt from a charity match between a UN XI and a Charity Aid Workers XI which is signed by Ban Ki-Moon, Mahmoud Ahmadinejad and Eddie Izzard. (I didn't play, I was just shouting abuse from the touchline. Fucking great.)

Have a fucking great night, pal.

All the best,
Malc x

_____

Sent on behalf of Malcolm Tucker
*

From : Malcolm Tucker [mailto: mtucker@gov.org.uk]
To : Sam Cassidy – Assistant to Malcolm Tucker
Subject :

Fuck me. That's scary. You actually sound like me.
*

From : Sam Cassidy – Assistant to Malcolm Tucker [mailto: scassidy@ gov.org.uk]
To : Malcolm Tucker
Subject :

I can forge your signature too. You'd better be nice to me.
S x

From : Toby Johnson [mailto: tobjohns23@aol.com]
To : Malcolm Tucker
Subject : Urgent

My name is Toby and I am twelve years old but please don't just dismiss what I'm saying because of that. I might be young but I'm not stupid.

My dad said I should email you because you are the real person who runs the country and not the Prime Minister.

I'm writing to you because I think the government should be doing more about climate change. It is a very big problem and you should be doing more. You need to have more cycle lanes and more trains and start making everyone drive electric cars and you need to do it NOW.

Please write back so I know you are going to do something and don't ignore me just because I am young.

Toby xxx
*

From : Malcolm Tucker [mailto: mtucker@gov.org.uk]
To : Sam Cassidy – Assistant to Malcolm Tucker
Subject :

Fuck off you precocious little shit. Go back to watching your Louis Theroux DVDs and learning to play Bob Marley songs on your acoustic guitar and crying with your dad at Up! and talking about how maybe you want to be a sculptor. To earn the right to talk to me you have to age 20 years, join the party, work your way up through the party, stand for election, secure a seat in the House of Commons, make a dazzling maiden speech and prove you have some intelligence about you and even then, when I do deign to talk to you, I'll only call you a cunt. If you're lucky. By then I may have found a more unpleasant word. Like ubercunt. Or cuntfuck. I dunno but I'm working on it …

Sam?
*

From : Sam Cassidy – Assistant to Malcolm Tucker [mailto: scassidy@gov.org.uk]
To : Malcolm Tucker
Subject : FW : RE : Urgent

Dear Toby,

Thank you very much for email. It's very exciting for me to receive correspondence from young people like yourself who are taking an interest in the world of politics. I totally agree with you, as does the Prime Minister and we are working as hard as we can to make these things happen.

Very best,
Malcolm Tucker

Sent on behalf of Malcolm Tucker
*

From : Malcolm Tucker [mailto: mtucker@gov.org.uk]
To : Sam Cassidy – Assistant to Malcolm Tucker
Subject : RE: FW: RE: Urgent

For once, I actually think you should have sent my one.

M x
*

From : Malcolm Tucker [mailto: mtucker@gov.org.uk]
To : Sam Cassidy – Assistant to Malcolm Tucker
Subject : Adam Boulton

Sam – can't sleep again. Can you rephrase this?

Adam,

I've just got a new HD TV and it makes you look like a ffunt – i.e. a fucking fat cunt.

I mean, you are a fucking fat cunt but still – is this really the image you want to project? You look like a fleshy bag of kettle chips. When I flipped over to Sky and saw your face I actually dry-heaved. A little bit of sick hit the back of my throat. It's ironic it's called Sky News because when you're doing an OB the last thing anyone's likely to see is the fucking sky. Basically, what I'm saying is you're so fat you could be mistaken for the giant canopy that envelopes our planet. My advice to you would be to get liposuction and use that vast residue of fat to sculpt a non-sentient Gollum-like sidekick to co-anchor the news with you. But then you've already got Kay Burley.

Oh, and you are a mindless mouthpiece for a tyrannical despot.

Kind Regards,

Malcolm
*

> **From :** Sam Cassidy – Assistant to Malcolm Tucker
> **To :** Malcolm Tucker
> **Subject :** RE : Adam Boulton
>
> Seems fine to me.
>
> S x
> *

> > **From :** Malcolm Tucker [mailto: mtucker@gov.org.uk]
> > **To :** Sam Cassidy – Assistant to Malcolm Tucker
> > **Subject :** RE: RE: Adam Boulton
> >
> > Great. I'll send as is.
> >
> > M x
> > *

BAD
MOTHER

" I would kick the living shit out of Colin Farrell "

London – March, 2010. The sky looks like a dirty, unmade bed. It's the kind of weather that makes you feel like you're in a Martin Amis novel. Threatening. Menacing. Brooding. Like a beaten wife contemplating revenge...

UCKER

I'M IN AN anonymous-looking black bullet of a car sleeking through Westminster on its way to Number Ten. And I am scared. Proper scared. Pant-wettingly, trickle-down-your-leg scared. Am I about to tell the Prime Minister some of our nuclear warheads have gone missing and fallen into the hands of a man who wears an eyepatch? No. Am I about to tell him a deadly virus caused by a mutation of Quorn is about to wipe out the nation's vegetarians? No. How about a meteor is about to smash into The London Eye at a speed of 18,000 miles per hour and the flash of light will (ironically) send all survivors blind? Nope.

I'm on my way to meet a guy and have a chat and do an interview. So why so scared? Well, I'm about to meet a very powerful man with a fearsome reputation. Not the Prime Minister – as we all know by now he has the reputation of being not very powerful and a little bit grumpy and mental. No, I'm on my way to meet Malcolm Tucker, the Chief Press

Officer for the Government of Great Britain and Northern Ireland, a man who is known for doing whatever it takes to get the job done. And for being a generally terrifying badaaasss sonofabitch. He is the Go To Guy. The Man Who Takes Care of Business. Famous for his brusque, take-no-prisoners approach and language his mum wouldn't be too proud of he is the man who keeps the back-benchers in line and the party on track, which considering how long this government has been around is no mean feat. He's the man who has been variously referred to as The Reaper, The Death Dealer, Mad Dog McFuck, Malcolm Nagasaki, Malcolm Tucker – Motherfucker and the man who put the Aaarrggggh! in PR. That's why I'm nervous.

As we slick through the wet streets my phone goes. I look at the screen. It's him. It's Malcolm Tucker. Calling me. My stomach plunges. I break out in a cold sweat. My heart races. Am I in trouble? Already? What have I done? Shit, now I know how all those hapless ministers must feel. I answer with some trepidation. 'Hello?' Silence. And then ... It's not Malcolm, it's his lovely assistant Sam. She's telling me Malcolm offers his massive apologies but he has to rearrange because, 'Something big's come up'. 'Probably a deadly virus or a meteor', I think to myself. A wave of relief surges over me. And then I think, 'Bugger. I have to go through all this again another day'.

Four days later, we're back on course. This time Malcolm is coming to us. With home field advantage I should feel slightly less nervous – but I don't. But then Malcolm breezes in, all smiles and matey banter and within five minutes I'm thinking the unthinkable – he's a really funny guy. Likeable. Nice even. Is it possible he's been completely misrepresented by the media all these years? Maybe it is. Maybe he is actually just a really great guy. Or maybe he's just as good at spin as they say he is and I've fallen for the schtick. But if it is schtick I have to say this is good schtick, man. Suddenly, I'm in The Matrix. I don't know what's reality and what isn't. I have a few minutes to collect my thoughts as Malcolm poses for a quick photo shoot, but then it's time for me to go all Bob Woodward on his ass. Here goes ...

How would you define your job as a spin doctor?

Well, most of the time I'm not a spin doctor, I'm a guy trying to undo spin. The media or the opposition will slant a story a certain way and I'm the guy who has to go, 'That's their spin – but that's not real, this is the reality'.

Is it a lonely job?

Yeah, sometimes. But I'm not going to go on a killing spree if that's what you're implying.

You've got this image of being one of the scariest men in Britain. A hard man, a psycho. How do you feel about that? And is it justified?

Look, that stuff is just a myth, you know? It's a media construct that some guy came up with – it made a good story and everyone's just run with it. I'm not a hard man. No way. And I should know – I grew up in Glasgow and there were plenty of hard men around. You know, you got the guys with the outlandish nicknames like, I dunno, Andy McStab and Peter 'Got My Own Incinerator' Irving. Then you got the guys with the tats. I knew this one guy who had the words 'FUCK YOU' etched into his teeth. True story. He actually had to beat the dentist up to get him to do it. He said he did it cos some girl had told him he had a welcoming smile and he thought that made him sound like a poof. So am I hard? Fuck no.

You're clearly a bit tasty though aren't you? Who'd win in a fight – Malcolm Tucker or Christopher Walken?

Well that's impossible to answer, right? It's completely hypothetical and I've never met him and don't know his background. Having said that, me. Obviously. The guy's got limbs like a Louise Bourgeois sculpture. It'd be like fighting Kiera Knightley on a diet. While she was dealing with a muscle-wasting disease. Which she contracted after spending a long time on the fucking Space Station.

Who'd win in a fight – Malcolm Tucker or Colin Farrell?

Me. Look, I'd like to reiterate I'm not a violent man. But I would kick the living shit out of Colin Farrell. But only because he deserves it.

OK, who'd win in a fight – Malcolm Tucker or Muhammad Ali?

Again, I'm not a violent man but ... me. I mean, I dance like a

> He's the man who has been variously referred to as The Reaper, The Death Dealer, Mad Dog McFuck, Malcolm Nagasaki, Malcolm Tucker – Motherfucker and the man who put the Aaarrggggh! in PR.

"What the fuck are you looking at?"

butterfly. And I sting like a tazer gun. Plus, you know, he's got Parkinsons.

Do you have any hobbies? Something to alleviate the pressure?

Yeah, I'm a serial killer. [Pause.] I'm kidding. Now you've got me fucking at it! [He laughs.]

You're very driven though aren't you? What was your childhood like?

My dad used to beat me. So did my mam. So did all the kids at school. When my parents let me go to school that is. They made me live in the chimney and I had to sleep standing up. Sometimes they'd hit me with a stick and make me do a noise like a crackling fire so they felt warm. If they didn't think it was good enough they'd set fire to my legs. I was in and out of hospital more often than the Carry On team. And that was before we reinvested in the health service so you'd often come out feeling worse than when you went in – because you'd contracted gangrene or TB. Aged five I was sniffing glue. Age six I was on the heroin. By the time I was 9 I was off the heroin but having to work 120 hours a week as a welder to pay back the drug debts. That's when the alcoholism and the gambling kicked in. No, you know what? Sorry to disappoint you, I had a lovely childhood. Nothing bad happened. I think I might have dropped a choc ice once.

How do you feel about the other parties? Do you have mates on the opposite side? Do you hang out together?

Honestly? No. I think they're

Malcolm "Nicknames" Tucker

He is Legend. His identities are protean. Here are just a handful:

The Gorbals Goebbels

Dr. Know

Malkiavelli

Pain Man

The Lying Scotsman

Malcolm X

The Sassenach Assassin

Lights Out

Horror House of Hammers

Shouty McKill

Double Tap

The Destroyer of Dreams

The Great White Motherfucker

The Punchdrunk Cunt

The Bastard

The Widow Maker

Davina

all evil fuckers. And I like people, I really do. But hang out with those wankers? I'd rather eat Sharon Osbourne's liposuction leftovers.

You've been in government a long time – have you ever thought about standing as an MP?

Yeah, it's crossed my mind of course. But it's just a mad impulse like contemplating suicide or wanting to push someone in a wheelchair off a bridge.

What do you see yourself doing when it all comes to an end?

Getting more serious about the serial killing. [Pause.] Actually, I'd like to get into laser eye surgery. I just like the idea of fucking with people's eyes. With lasers. Or – I could just give it all up. Lie on the sofa and grow my fingernails really long until I can play my acoustic guitar in the next room without getting up.

When it's all said and done what do you want written on your headstone?

Morbid. I like it. 'I can't talk right now – fuck off'. Or 'Kiss my decomposing arse'. I don't know. Maybe something more moving and inspirational.

FuckMan:
Able to crush weak egos at a single glance

Tucker. Malcolm Tucker.
On Her Majesty's motherfucking Secret Service.

Have you ever been offered the part of a baddie in a movie?

I was offered the part of a hit man in a British gangster movie but I said no.

Why?

It was a British gangster movie.

Are you so scary that you've actually scared yourself?

What kind of fucking question is that?

A shit one. Sorry! If you could change one thing about the world what would it be?

Fuck me, what is this – Newsround? I don't know. Persuade everyone to see the world in the same reasoned, enlightened way as me? Does that sound up myself? If it does then just put – go back in time and assassinate Hitler and Clarkson. Actually, that could be a lot of fun. A time travelling

hit man. I should pitch that to someone.

So you're still running the show?

The PM's running the show. I'm merely Morgan Freeman to his Batman.

WE EXPECTED MALCOLM to want 'approval' on our copy but amazingly he didn't look to edit us at all. But, ironically, we ended up censoring ourselves because we were too scared to run some of our ideas past him.

Here are some of the photo shoot ideas that we didn't even pitch to Malcolm.

FUCK MAN
Special powers :

Ability to stop criminals in their tracks by stunning them with graphic abuse about shoving shopping trolleys up your granny's … er …

'trolleyholder'.

Death stare. Curdles your insides at 1000 paces.

Super Shoutyness. Can shout so loud your eardrums explode. Not only do you go deaf you immediately fall over from loss of balance. And shit yourself. Probably.

ON HER MAJESTY'S MOTHERFUCKING SERVICE.

MALVERINE.

THE PHYSICAL IMPOSSIBILITY OF MALCOLM IN THE MIND OF SOMEONE LIVING.

10
Weird Westminster Rumours About Malcolm Tucker

1. He once threatened the King of Spain with a plate of berenjenas gratinadas.

2. He has his own network of secret tunnels that he uses to get round Westminster.

3. Remember how Leslie Grantham killed that taxi driver years ago? Malcolm was behind it.

4. He likes to eat onion and garlic sandwiches to make his breath stink so people feel even more disorientated while he's bollocking them.

5. He once arranged a meeting with a back-bencher who disagreed with him. After a long chat the back-bencher booked an appointment with Dignitas. He wasn't even ill.

6. He has a special app on his phone which tracks the location of all MPs at all times.

7. He once badly beat up a female Minister with his erect penis.

8. He was in the Twin Towers when the planes hit and carried on with a conference call with the DTI till he felt they had discussed everything they needed to.

9. Actors like Christian Bale and Javier Bardem have asked to meet him for advice on how to look scary.

10. He's had fifteen heart attacks but never talks about them.

*?!**£?!!*****

From : Andrew Jackson [mailto : ajackson@ladsmag.com]
To : Malcolm Tucker [mailto : mtucker@gov.org.uk]
Subject : The spread

Hi Malc,

Here's the interview and photoshoot as it stands. Any changes you
want let me know. Btw, you still want me to pretend I don't know you?
I think it would read fine if I had a line in it saying we know each other
from college days. I don't think it alters the content/ how you come
across.

From : Malcolm Tucker [mailto : mtucker@gov.org.uk]
To : Andrew Jackson [mailto : ajackson@ladsmag.com]
Subject : Re : The spread

No, you don't know me. And yeah. I want some fucking changes. But you
knew that already. I'll call you in five.

Glenn – to be abs clear, I want 4th sector to be about RADICAL CHANGE. Find the ppl who can drive this forward. Get their input. How many potential for soc. mob. be tapped? Poss questions: WHO? WHAT? WHERE? WHEN? HOW? HOW MUCH? ETZ.
Nicola

P.S WHY? WHY NOT? WHY NOW?

4th SECTOR MEMO

From: **Glenn Cullen**
To: **Terri Coverley, Oliver Reeder**

This is a covering message to confirm that I am herewith sending each of you a copy of the summary of the initial research into the viability of the proposed Departmental Initiative commissioned by the Secretary of State, hereby known as "The Fourth Sector Initiative", a copy of which has been furnished separately to the Secretary of State.

As the aforementioned note indicates, this discharges the initial research period. I am forwarding this note to allow for due consideration and discussion to take place. Meanwhile I shall be undertaking Phase Two of the initial research, much of which I shall, for reasons of efficiency and ease of co-ordination, be conducting out of the office for a few days commencing Thursday. Due to the intensity of the proposed research and various geographical logistics I will be checking emails only between 13:00 and 13:40 and again between 15:40 and 16:00. I will be back in the office on Monday 23rd.

Glenn Cullen

From : Ollie [mailto : oliverreeder@dosac.gov.uk]
To : Glenn [mailto : glenncullen@dosac.gov.uk]
cc : Nicola [mailto : nicolamurray@dosac.gov.uk]
Subject: **Glenn - Didn't You Have Tickets For The Trent Bridge Test That Starts This Thursday?**

And did you generate your 'covering message' using one of those online bullshit algorithms? I think I speak for everyone when I say how much we all admire your own social mobility.
Ollie

*

From : Terri [mailto : terricoverley@dosac.gov.uk]
To : Glenn [mailto : glenncullen@dosac.gov.uk]
cc : Nicola [mailto : nicolamurray@dosac.gov.uk]
Subject: **clarification please!**

I hate to be the experienced, sceptical communications professional here, but I don't understand what this is about. If I am to work up what we call a coherent narrative for the media, I need some 'positives'! Some 'good news'! As it stands, we have a potential policy which seems to be universally disliked! I mean, I'm NOT a politician. But surely Glenn's feedback says it all. Everybody hates it AND they don't know what it means. Hope this is useful,
Terri.

*

From : Nicola [mailto : nicolamurray@dosac.gov.uk]
To : Glenn [mailto : glenncullen@dosac.gov.uk]
cc : Terri [mailto : terricoverley@dosac.gov.uk], Ollie [mailto : oliverreeder@dosac.gov.uk]
Subject : **Cunt Amnesty**

For fuck's sake. Glenn, did you go out of your way to find the most unhelpful and nasty people to ask? Did you actually even SPEAK to anyone? Some of these quotes from people sound a lot like YOU being cynical e.g "This is bollocks. If we're planning to patronise people on housing estates, civil war would involve less fucking paperwork..." Or "Oh goody. A maypole in every community!" Or "What about declaring a Cunt Amnesty? Communities could hand in their anti-social cunts and get, I don't know, methadone vouchers..."

EVERYONE! I want us to move on from seeking feedback. Move forward. Start pushing people into supporting a very meaningful initiative. Think microbanking...think Big Picture with each community a village-size pixel...food clubs...allotments allotments ALLOTMENTS...old respecting young + vice versa...engaged, reciprocated community policing...street identities (Ollie, could every street have its own website, in theory?)...bakeries cf France... community/national service...job swaps, car shares, the list is endless. Come on!
Nicola

*

From : Glenn [mailto : glenncullen@dosac.gov.uk]
To : Malcolm [mailto : mtucker@gov.org.uk]
Subject : **Fourth Sector**

Malcolm – Fourth Sector stuff so far. I'm afraid she's gone up like a balloon on this one. She's got a look in her eyes like she's Sinatra at the moment. She firmly believes in flying this Department to the Moon and letting it play among the stars regardless of their colour, creed or sexual identity. What should we do?
Best, Glenn

*

From : Malcolm [mailto : mtucker@gov.org.uk
To : Ollie [mailto : oliverreeder@dosac.gov.uk]
cc : Ollie [mailto : oliverreeder@dosac.gov.uk], Glenn [mailto : glenncullen@dosac.gov.uk], Terri [mailto : terricoverley@dosac.gov.uk]
Subject : Fourth Sector

Attention: stop thinking about the Fourth Fucking Sector before one of you says something stupid (e.g anything) in the real world and turns DOSAC into the Cabinet version of fucking Mr BLOBBY. Just shut the fuck up. I'm coming over in the morning to punch the press release repeatedly. Punch it and punch it until it's just a shapeless, formless, inoffensive fucking CORPSE.
I want it to say nothing, to promise nothing, to have no spending implications and to be of no fucking interest whatsoever to anyone.
Punching you already,
Malcolm.

BRIEFING NOTE
From the desk of Terri Coverley, DOSAC Head of Press.
Contact details below.

EMBARGO: Suggest for immediate use.
STATUS: Awaiting final clearance by MT.

'FOURTH SECTOR' INITIATIVE LAUNCHED BY DOSAC

A new grassroots initiative to release the untapped potential of ordinary people through engagement in their own communities has been announced by Nicola Murray, Secretary of State for Social Affairs and Citizenship.

The Fourth Sector programme will explore ways of transforming areas of high deprivation by empowering local people, whose energy and talents will be guided by inspirational citizens known as Fourth Sector Pathfinders.

Commenting on the initiative, Nicola Murray said "I am thrilled to be spearheading what I hope will be a landmark policy for DOSAC. "

NOTE TO EDITORS: A more detailed explanation of the Fourth Sector Initiative will be issued in due course.

In the coming weeks DOSAC will be exploring opportunities for cross-sector synergy with local agencies and stakeholders including local government, their service partners and private sector contractors, local media, voluntary and charitable bodies and community representatives. The framework for this consultation will be announced soon, following a period of pre-consultation with potential consultants.

ends

terricoverley@dosac.gov.uk

Part 1

Malcolm Tucker's Guide on How To Use A Focus Group

Are focus groups helpful? In a word : absofuckinglutelynot. Fuck no. As a famous man once said : There are lies, damned lies and fucking cunting focus groups. The problem is focus groups are made up of members of the public and are therefore intrinsically unreliable / lop-sided / racist / mental. They are also 'run' by marketing 'people' for 'the purposes of qualitative research'. In other words, it's the mad leading the mad creating a feedback loop of fizzing shit. Plus, putting a bunch of people with nothing better to do in an airless basement can't end well. At best, you'll get a Downfall parody you can put on the net with the other 4 trillion Downfall parodies. At worst, the white noise that is people's 'opinion' will drive you insane until you genuinely believe the room you are in has become some kind of Stargate and opened a portal to hell.

So. How do you get the 'best' from these fucking Am-Dram travesties of a bad Sartre play?

- Firstly, DO NOT listen to one person in particular - EVEN IF THEY AGREE WITH YOU. ONE PERSON IS NOT REPRESENTATIVE OF ANYTHING. EVEN IF THEY AGREE WITH YOU. IMPORTANT : YOU ARE ALSO NOT REPRESENTATIVE OF ANYTHING. YOUR VIEWS ARE UNIMPORTANT. REMEMBER THAT.

- If there is no consensus then IGNORE EVERYTHING EVERYONE SAYS.

- If there is a consensus then LISTEN to that consensus and ask yourself the following question : IS IT MAD?

- If it isn't mad then GIVE IT SERIOUS CONSIDERATION. After you have given it serious consideration REJECT IT OUT OF HAND. The purpose of a focus group is TO GIVE THE ILLUSION THAT WE ARE LISTENING. It is NOT TO FORM POLICY. Otherwise, that group of people in that airless basement picking their noses and stirring their cups of polystyrene tea with discarded rectal applicators would be the Cabinet and not A RANDOM BUNCH OF SKIN-BAGS WITH THE MENTAL DEXTERITY OF A JENGA BLOCK.

To help save time, here are a couple of 'types' you can write off straightaway.

1. Motorway Man. He spends a lot of time on a motorway. So what THE FUCK is he going to tell us exactly? How important it is for the country to invest in bigger glove compartments? That the baked beans left under the hot plate at Newport Pagnell tend to go 'a bit solid'. This guy is – by definition – out of touch. You might as well ask the opinion of Jumped Under A Train Woman or Been Working On The International Space Station For The Last Four Years Guy.

2. Holby City Woman. She watches Holby City. She is a human vacuum.

3. The Disillusioned Voter. AKA The Grumpy Cunt. This guy is pissed off about everything. The immigrants. The economy. The NHS. The roads. Erectile dysfunction. The

fact that he's just won the lottery. The fact that he's a grumpy cunt. The fact that despite being a grumpy cunt he wasn't invited on Grumpy Old Cunts even though Will Self was. He's got a point on the last one – but you can ignore the rest.

4. The Young Person Who Went Straight From School to Working in a Key-cutters. Highly unlikely to have an opinion on anything unless it features in their tiny world. "I think they should put the Post Office back at the end of my road because now I have to walk for ten minutes. And there must be a lot of people in that position." "What, there must be a lot of people in the position of living in your road?" "... Yeah ..." No idea what's going on in the world. Gets all his / her information from things mates have said in the pub. Probably thinks you can get herpes if you put your hand too far into a ballot box.

5. The Student. Basically there in the hope of free biscuits and Red Bull.

6. The Woman Who Will Agree with Everything That is Said Because That is What She Thinks You Want. Or Because She Doesn't Really Understand What is Being Said and By Agreeing With it She Hopes it Will Go Away.

7. The Fucking Guardian Reader. If you want to know what a Guardian reader thinks you can read The Guardian. Plus, that way, you get a crossword.

8. The Fucking Telegraph Reader. A ruddy-faced village idiot who looks like he's directly descended from Lord Melchett in Blackadder II.

9. The Local Business Man. Only interested in issues concerning local business, more specifically the business local to him.

10. Dot Cotton's Younger, Less Glamorous Sister. She's really only there for a bit of company and she's not paying attention to what's being said because she's desperate for a fag break.

11. The Fucking Weirdo Who Says Stuff Either Too Quiet or Too Loud Which Doesn't Make Sense and Trails off into Nothing or Ends Mid-Thought Thereby Making Everyone Feel Uncomfortable. Ignore them. Unless they're in charge of the focus group. In which case fire the fucker.

Of course these caricatures are not to be taken too seriously. MEMORISE THEM NOW.

Other broader points to bear in mind:

- The Under 30s are too young to know anything.

- People between the ages of 30 and 40 are only interested in stuff that pertains directly to them / their newborn children.

- The Over 40s are losing their faculties and no longer able to absorb and process information properly.

- And remember : People talk shit. They talk even more shit when they are asked to manufacture opinions on subjects they are totally ignorant of and /or couldn't give a gnat's anus about.

Happy Focus Grouping!

Part 2

Malcolm Tucker's Advice on How To Behave in Public and Private

---

Public

Some tips on standards expected of ministers in their public behaviour.

War Memorials

When at a war memorial during a service of remembrance amusing thoughts will occur to you. What might the President of France look like with a melon on his dong? If you had to, which finance minister would you gobble last? Do not pass these on to whoever is standing next to you. If you feel you might be unable to stop yourself smiling - imagine your own cock being fed into a moulinex. Clinton once coaxed a tear this way in Normandy.

Travel

Try to get a snap of you on the tube or bus early on in your ministerial career. After that. Cars. Government fucking cars. Everywhere. I don't want your papers left on a train and I don't want a nuclear tactical strike on N. Korea delayed cos you're fiddling with your u-lock outside Kennington Tube okay?

Verboten Activity

Over the years the British civil service has drawn up a list of activities unbecoming to a UK Government Minister. Now you are a minister you may no longer engage in:

- Krazy golf
- Visiting pound shops
- Running with the bulls in Pamplona
- Construction of conceptual art
- Dancing
- Polo / croquet / deer stalking
- The wearing of hats at jaunty angles
- Falling over

Some of them may appear to be arbitrary or harsh. I don't know why regular golf is allowed but krazy golf is suspended as an activity for your time in office. I do not make the rules. I merely sniff the culture and tell you what is permissible.

Private

The Government and its communications officers strongly support your right to a private life. Up to a point. Basically, you should have a right to expect that anything you do in your private life should remain private - unless you are doing anything that you would wish to keep private. At which point the right is waived.

Fucking et al
You may fuck.

However:
- Do not fuck dead shit
- Do not fuck in a hat
- In fact – avoid all varieties of weird fucking
- NB, gay fucking is not weird fucking, it is fine fucking– so long as you are gay. If you are doing gay fucking and you are not gay it is weird fucking.

One-Offs
- Try to be a considerate lover. Newsflash: blowing your beans over someone's dress is not mutually satisfactory intercourse. An unsatisfied lover is more likely to blab.
- When a one-off comes out make sure there's no eye-catching details to

emerge: Harlequins away strip/carrots up the pipehole/shouting Schnell! Schnell! at your moment of climax etc.

- Public attitudes have changed over the years but you may like to know what sexual activities are considered 'too much' by focus groups: Tea-bagging; Rimming; Badgering; Dogging; Gradgrinding; the Slippery Boot; Bear Baiting. There also appears to be only limited acceptability in the South West for Felching.

Affairs

- When choosing a mate for the deception of your life partner and family – don't fuck down the tree (DFDT). Pick a fellow adulterer at or above your own level. Researchers are easy. But for a more relaxing adultery you need someone who's also going to be fucked if it comes out you're fucking. Check Government, BBC and Civil Service websites for Ministers, Senior Civil Servants or journalists at or above your level you might find attractive.

Dicking About on Yachts

As a Government Minister rich men will try to make friends with you. This is not due to your wide knowledge of the Regional Development Agency 'rejigs' of the early noughties. Or because you look hot in those speedoes.

They want your cock in a box / tits in a jar.

Here is a good rule of thumb. If you want to meet some millionaire cunt, ask yourself would I be doing this if we had to meet in the Rainforest Café on the M54 Westbound to Telford at 7.50am on a Wednesday in November?

Or is it cos it's June at the Cup Final/on his yacht with Naomi Campbell and some fuck from Snow Patrol that it seems so important to talk to him?

Part 3

Malcolm Tucker's Guide to Managing Your Public Image

How to Speak in Public

Firstly and most obviously – don't fall over, vomit, defile yourself, burst into flame or say anything overtly racist / sexist / anti-disabled / anti-religion and /or likely to incite violence. So, no rhetorical flourishes involving 'rivers of blood' or 'valleys of haematoma' or 'tsunamis of nun-chucks'. Also, and I hope this goes without saying, no swearing.

Secondly, and equally importantly, don't try to be funny. Being funny is very hard. Even being mildly amusing is hard. Look at Adrian Chiles.

On a related note, do not try to 'be human' or 'show some personality'. People don't like personality. Oh they say they do. But they really don't. What they actually want is someone very, very bland who instead of having a personality offers a vacuum – a blank canvas – on to which you can project your own idea of what that person's personality might be. Look at Adrian Chiles.

Don't try to be Obama. I've not served with Obama, I don't know Obama, Obama is not a friend of mine. But take it from me, you're no Obama. Keep hand gestures to a minimum. I don't want to see your impression of

Shiva working a Diablo while doing a Rubik's cube. Don't wave your arms in the air like you don't care. People are looking to you for guidance. You need to look sensible and in charge. You need to look like someone who keeps their arms firmly OUT of the air because they DO CARE. You do not want to look like a human wind machine. Which, is of course, what you actually are.

- **Don't point.** It's rude and it will lead to a photograph in which it looks like you are giving a Nazi salute.

- **No Nazi salutes.**

- **Don't sniff.** It'll look like you've been doing coke.

- **Don't let your nose run either.** It'll look like you've been doing coke.

- **Don't swallow or gulp.** It'll look like you're lying. And you've been doing coke.

- **Don't sweat.** Ever. You may want to consider elective surgery whereby you have the nerves to your armpits severed. If you do go down the cosmetic surgery route you can also consider having botox. Having your face paralysed makes it harder for people to tell when you're lying.

- **Don't repeatedly touch your nose** or stroke your ear or rub your chin or play with your hair – it looks like you're somehow trying to wank your face off.

- **Use short sentences.** It's been scientifically proven that the general public will give politicians 3.8 seconds before they're bored.

- **Don't use posh words** like 'milieu' or 'rapprochement'. You don't sound clever, you sound like a cunt.

- **Don't say 'er' or 'um'.** Say things that make you sound dynamic and important. Like, 'Look'. And, 'Listen'.

- **Don't modulate your voice.** I don't want to hear a warble like Whitney fucking Houston before the crack kicked in. Try to speak in a monotone. If you accidentally say something controversial people might not notice.

- **Don't let your throat get too dry.** If you get too dry you start to sound like you've got throat cancer.

- **Don't let your throat get too wet.** You'll end up drenching your audience like Roy Hattersley or Annie Sprinkle.

- **Maintain sustained eye contact** – but don't go creepy with it. You want to aim for the look of a diligent air-traffic controller. Not a mad, starey rapist.

- **Try to sound normal** without actually saying anything that a normal person might say.

- **Don't be boring.**

- **Don't be interesting.**

- **Don't be too general.**

- **Don't be too personal.**

- **Don't say ANYTHING** that isn't approved by the Communications team.

- **Look confident.**

- **Don't – FOR THE LOVE OF GOD – look over-confident.**

- **Above all be relaxed.**

- **And, finally**, if public speaking makes you nervous try the following techniques:

    Breathing exercises.

    Beta-blockers.

    Resignation.

How to Stage a Photoshoot

As you'll all be aware our Secretary of State for the Department of Social Affairs and Citizenship, Nicola Murray, was recently utterly (and unfairly) humiliated by the august institution that is the Great British Press. In layman's terms, they tipped a big bucket of hot bollocks over her head. For those of you who don't remember she was photographed in front of a poster supporting our candidate Liam Bentley in the Leamington by-election which the press chose to crop so that it looked like she was standing in front of the words 'I AM BENT'.

This was highly unfortunate and, of course, in no way a reflection of Nicola's competence or lack of as a (new) Minister. There but for the grace of god go we, right? However, there are a number of important lessons to be learnt here:

1. Journalists are the enemy.
2. Photographers are the enemy.
3. Anything we can be photographed next to is also the enemy.
4. The entire physical universe is a minefield of unexploded gaffes and visual faux pas that could explode at any time. The entire physical universe is the enemy.

Remember: the press will fuck you over in a heartbeat. So, keep your eyes open and your brain switched on. You need to be alert at all times. Like Jason Bourne on Ritalin.

To illustrate how many pitfalls there are out there I'm throwing out a few random examples to watch for.

Nicola has shown her customary good humour throughout and – great credit to her – has very sportingly agreed to let the IT boys use her as a visual aid in the following examples. So, thanks and kudos to Nicola without whom the following wouldn't be happening.

First off, watch out for words that can be cropped.

I hope you're all smart enough to avoid being snapped next to a big sign saying, 'Massive Hypocrite Here Today'. But what about words hidden within other words? In this example, Nicola wasn't clever enough.

One obvious thing to watch for is words that seem particularly apposite for politicians. Obvious examples would be : liar, fraud, charlatan, weasel, bastard.

Or look out for words appropriate to you as an individual. In this example, the press have isolated what they see as one of Nicola's defining characteristics.

Another perfectly innocent looking scenario.

Another PR disaster for Nicola.

Of course, in real life, Nicola would have learnt her lesson by now.

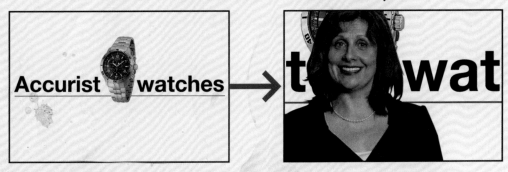

But, for training purposes, here she is making the same mistake over and over again.

Here are a couple more :

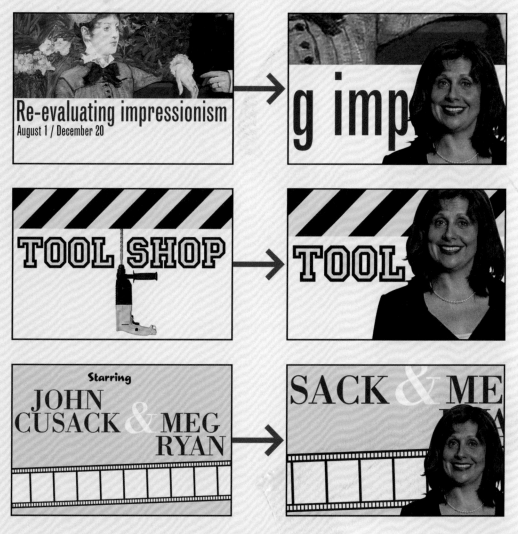

I could reprint various posters featuring the word 'countryside' but you've got the idea.

A Guide to TV Interviews

Sooner or later you will do a live TV interview. You will arrive at the studio where a girl who looks about 15 wearing a headset and carrying a clipboard will rush you down some corridors, saying "We're travelling" into a walkie-talkie.

You will be made up by a chatty woman who'll tell you indiscreet gossip about Robson Green and then you'll be there, suddenly, in the studio, in the chair, the hot lights burning you, millions watching you, the questions flying.

This is how you handle it:

Presenters

Paxman: He is still the daddy. You can't beat him. When cocky youngsters occasionally try he slaps them down, steals their wallet, fucks their wife and buys a new fridge with their Mastercard.

Gavin Esler: Seems reasonable. People breathe a sigh of relief when they know it's going to be Nice Smiley Gavin and not Death Mask of Shergar Paxman. Dont be fooled. He fucked George Galloway so hard his wee two-tone beard fell off and he had to sell his shares in fucking Halliburton and Nestlé to get a transplant. Tread carefully.

Kirsty Wark: She's cleverer than you are, okay? Do not forget this or she will make you look like a dribbling chimp with a 2:2 from Loughborough wanking in a tyre to the theme tune from Mr Benn. You're a professional politician, right? You just know about politics. That's all you've ever thought about or cared about because if it wasn't you wouldn't be doing this job, you abnormal fucking freak of nature. Kirsty though, she knows about politics, sure she does, but she also knows about fucking opera and fucking art and fucking Japanese Noh Theatre and films and books and all of that shit that other people get passionate about, but which just make you reach for the fucking Hansard and a Tunnock's wafer.

Kay Burley: Being interviewed by Kay is, as we all know, like being interviewed by a backward child. That's obviously great most of the time. But occasionally she will throw you a curveball like a child might – "Why is there war?" "What is Europe?" – and if you can't answer it's you who ends up looking like the thick-as-pigshit chancer.

Adam Boulton: I know you want to laugh, but don't. Really. It just reflects badly on you. Try to pretend he doesn't look like a male Sandi Toksvig with a glandular complaint. (Oh, and you know I sometimes say that you should imagine an interviewer naked in order not to be intimidated? For the love of Christ don't do this with Adam.)

Body language

Look attentive and engaged. No crossed legs. No touching the face. No touching the cock. Don't fold arms. Don't look away when thinking of an answer. Breathe normally. Don't shit yourself. Answer immediately. Don't cough. No stuttering. Don't sniff. Blink between 5 and 7 times a minute - no more or less. Maintain eye contact at all times. Make sure you consciously do or don't do all of the above but YOU MUST MAKE SURE you don't look like you're consciously doing or not doing them. And above all be relaxed.

Yes and no

In answer to a question that blatently requires an affirmative or negative response, you may be tempted by the old-school 'start talking reasonably without saying yes or no' gambit. For example:

INTERVIEWER: "Will you cut the money available to hospices? Yes or no?"

YOU: "We have been working closely, and will continue to work closely, with the hospice movement, and Sir Peter Dudderidge himself has said that in real terms the funding..."

You're a cunt, right there. You may as well stop speaking now, everyone hates you. Your mum's watching, she's thinking "What a fuckwad, wish I'd taken

Karen's advice, got rid of him at 24 weeks and taken that job doing PR at House Of Fraser".

Everyone knows you're avoiding the question. How is that a good thing? You think you're kidding them? You think people are going "Well he's making noises with his mouth, that's enough for us"? The public are stupid, they are not dead.

You answer a yes or no question with a 'yes' or a 'no'. Okay? Then you say the things you want to say. Yeah? That's when you can trot out all the dissembling and the misrepresentation and the half-truths and the distortions because you've earned them with a yes or a no.

Always think, if asked a 'yes or no-ey' - "Michael Howard. Do I want to look like Michael Howard". That always works.

Because the bottom line is always, in a live TV interview, DO NOT LOOK LIKE MICHAEL FUCKING HOWARD.

Malc – this was on Emma's Macbook, thought you might like it. And therefore, like me, more, for getting hold of it. Maybe not like me, as such, Just not, I'm not suggesting you need to ... it's just, you know, I sometimes feel you have such, well contempt for me Malcolm, and scorn, beyond what would be considered reasonable considering what I ... Oh, I don't know, sorry, it's just my self esteem has taken some real knocks lately.

Cheers !!

Ollie

CONFIDENTIAL

Memo from Emma Messinger

re: PETER MANNION IMAGE etc.
To: James Edwards, Alison Wright, Sophie Anderson
cc: Stewart Pearson

Dear James, Alison, Sophie

Stewart has asked me to do an assessment of Peter's image, and what we can do to change it if we feel we need to.

Ha! I'm joking! Of course we need to, the man's a fashion disaster. It's like Al-Qaeda blew up Next.

First off – this is a CONFIDENTIAL document. No-one outside of we four and Stewart must see this. Peter, in particular, must never see it.

contd. overleaf

Peter's 'style'

Peter's natural style is 'traditional' - Gieves & Hawkes suits, Church's shoes, haircut at Trumpers, prostitute in Shepherd's Market, pissed at the Carlton Club, home in a black cab.

I was joshing about Shepherd's Market. It's Dean Street.

He sort of stopped thinking about clothes in any meaningful way in the 1980s. Hence the double-breasted suits, the hair, the braces, the whole Robert-Palmer-on-a-speedboat-sponsored-by-Dunhill vibe.

Hair

It's floppy. Women used to like this, apparently, mainly due to the beautiful young boys in those 80s things like Maurice and Brideshead and a Room With A View. Note though - beautiful young boys. Peter is no longer any of those words. Floppy hair with angular cheekbones = sexy. Floppy hair with floppy face = a lesbian James May.

We need to get Peter to go much shorter - French crop, brushed forward. It'll make him look younger, hide the grey more. Tell him he'll look like Clooney (Alison, can you tell him this? He'll know I'm taking the piss.)

Clothes

Stewart's tried to get him into Ozwald Boateng and he's not averse, but he always tends to go back to his double-breasted pinstripe monstrosities. He looks like he's playing an estate agent in Ashes To Ashes.

Again – Alison, Sophie, tell him how 'suave' he looks in the Boetang suits, tell him they're 'slimming'. They're not - a fat man is a fat man is a fatty fatty fat man whatever he wears - I don't want to get into a personal sidebar here, but in my view weight control is simply a matter of self discipline and those who fail to maintain it are weak.

But anyway, shoes

Obviously, the Church's are fine with a suit. But what about weekends? What about when a story breaks on a Sunday - a train crash (often in midlands, don't know why) or an earthquake in Mexico or someone famous and ancient pegs it - and they go to Peter at his farmhouse and want an on-camera statement? He needs some good checked shirts (Ted Baker), jeans (no stonewashed, however much he begs) and, I would suggest, black Converse Hi-Tops.

Now this will be a problem. I can hear him now: "Plimsoles!? You want me to wear plimsoles!? 'Pumps'?! Let me tell you, I haven't done PE since the fifth form, and I'm certainly..." Etcetera, blah blah, you know how he bangs on, like a particularly uninspired issue of Private Eye. So, again, we need to talk him down. Tell him McCartney wears them, Bill Nighy, Sting, Monty Don, those guys.

Personality

In interviews and public appearances, can we work on getting him to be less Leslie Phillips? All that "I say, steady on, ding dong, hello ladies" business. It's the 21st century, even where he lives in Hampshire.

Peter needs to be straighter, more middle-class-blokey, you know? Like he knows what wine to order, but can also change an indicator bulb and talk about John Terry. More "I'm just an ordinary honest guy trying to get my common-sense point across" - that's the kind of false image he needs to adopt.

Oh, and he should definitely say 'guy' more, rather than 'man'. He talked in an interview last week about a 'black man'. Not good. Sounded like Cecil Rhodes. It's 'black guy', it's 'gay guy', it's 'young guy'. These are basics.

Finally: weight

I alluded to this briefly above. We are a young party. We are, on the whole, a slim party. Peter is not fitting into this demographic. We can't make him younger, sadly, so let's get him on the Atkins. It's the only diet men can do without feeling like you've chopped their cocks off. It will also mean he'll have to give up the bottle and a half of Merlot a night, which will be good for a) his big red drunkard's face and b) not being such a cunt in morning meetings.

Okay, those are my thoughts. Your turn now to chip in. Remember - be as harsh as you like, Peter won't see any of this.

Best

Emma

Sam —
Could you fax this to
Peter Mannion's private
number please?

Ta
Malc.

OLLIE— Thank your 'Squeezy dumpling', Emma
for the great photos of Stewart's mood board.
I particularly like what Mannion's minions have done
to fill it — as does the Daily Mirror —— M

FAO: BLUE PETER GREEN Emma RED PHIL MY RAINBOW ALLIANCE !!!

I'm off the radar until Weds — when I return I want to see this MOODBOARD refilled with your your your

(I've given you some e.g.s...)

MEME TROPES

ASTONISH ME!

(+) (−)

POSITIVE/CORRECT/THE FUTURE ON RIGHT

NEGATIVE/WRONG/OUT OF DATE ON LEFT

'Q' AS ADJECTIVE

'Q' AS PASSIVE VERB

NUDGE

'S.A.C.'

PUSH DRIVE

'DOUGHSACK'

FUDGE

*'UPGRADE'

PAEDOPHOBIA

'LOL'

'X'

*'FIXING THE IS-BROKE' → ISMPHOBIA

AMENDMENT

REDACTION

STRAIGHT/CROOKED

WAR ON 'ERROR'

GAY/JOHN LEWIS FARM SHOPS?

POLICY ESSENCES:
e.g SOCIAL ARCHITECTURE not SOCIAL ENGINEERING

GOVT →

CHANGE! MORE c.f THIS (HQ)

CHINA →
FIXED BORDERS →
BUTCH

RETROFITTED CHIC PRE-MODERNISM

BRITAIN PLUS
PROGNOSIST

BRITAIN
DENIALIST

TRAINERS LEADERS
FINDERS KEEPERS
COLE COWELL

ULSTER →
PAGE BLEED →
FEM

STUBBORN POLICY STRAINS:
'care', 'regulate'
'subsidise', 'ban'
'fair', 'govern'

FLIMSY
MIMSY
WHIMSY = #FAIL

FAO: BLUE PETER GREEN EMMA RED PHIL WE DE 'COLOURED PEOPLE' MASSA?

I'm disappearing up my own fucking ARSE. Instead of THOUGHT BUBBLES

please accept my [BUM GRAPES]

ASTONISH ME

DILEMMA:
A: 'Shock astonish' or B: 'delight astonish'

If A: CAPITAL PUNISHMENT (Swot)
If B: HIGH STREET 'LISTENING BOOTHS' (Phil)

FACT: BEARDS MAKE MOUTHS LOOK LIKE VAGINAS

APATHY/D.C./LOCAL AUTHORITIES - NO
'SPOTIFY/MARVEL/WARLORDS - YES
GUM/LITTER/CHAV TV - NO
PETS FOR PENSIONERS - YES

WIDER COMMUNITY? FAT COCKS? BIG ARSES? LARGE SCOTCH?
Yes WE CAN BE NICE!

MEME = ME + ME

TATTOOINE [X] ENDOR [✓]

'FLAT WHITE'

MORE PICTURES NO / MORE PEOPLE YES

(SPIT)
CUT...
Putting the 'rope' in 'Europe' in my...

STEWART (cc PETER)
let the record show!
reluctantly did the
Photoshopping for Peter
I was literally following
orders. (Phil)

Yummy Daddies

Zeitgeist Macht Frei

...LETTER!

There was a young girl from Denver
whose breasts were of different sizes
One was so small
It was nothing at all)
But the other was big and won prizes

Peter -
Please stop this arsing about? You need to ok those drafts

For Hannah ✓

Do you even understand what a moodboard IS bitch?

It's not some ADMIN RESOURCE
This is so NOT what Stewart intended. ok ☺

Shit! Thanks for that Emma. Just sorted drafts for H. Fuck me this is better than the one in front of me P

Peter it's INTRANET.
And Emma, why don't you stop clogging up things

PHIL - For your eyes only:
Cleaner has complained for 3rd time about you doing weird things at night in Peter's office. Says Shelyer nearly had heart attacks, she won't clear 'it' up in the future. And Peter's spare suit doesn't even fit you properly. E

Primary School Rules!

0-9 & £ $0

From: Nicola Murray
To: Frank Hutcheson

Frank

Herewith a taster for the 'magnum opus'. Still experimenting with style and tone. Vitally important that the 'real human Nicola' shines through. Also, v. imp that I come across as wanting to help the disadvantaged in our society, not to lecture them!

I'd be enormously grateful if you could give me any thoughts you have, Frank. Not just as a publisher but as a friend. I've got a relatively easy stretch at the Dept coming up, if I did some serious bunking off I could get a first draft (c.70k words?) to you by Sept?

Be great to catch up – LUNCH! SOON! – not just to talk about the book/fee etc (obv exciting though) but to GOSSIP. I have DINED OUT on that story you told me about Christopher Hitchens – and to think he's got away with it for all these years! Honestly Frank, is it silly of me? We've met socially only twice but it feels like we've known each other for YONKS.

So, let me know any initial 'ballpark guidelines' – length, timetable, awful business of money – ASAP and I'll heave the trusty AirBook into the orangery and get cracking!

Best wishes,

Nicola xx

Secretary of State for Social Affairs and Citizenship

PS. Ooh, ooh! Why not come to my World Class Communities drinks do on the 24th? Honestly Frank, the world of social mobility attracts a LOT of gay 'movers and shakers'. If you're interested I could introduce you to some hot pairs of socially mobile trousers ha ha! x

ROBINSON PUBLISHING

Dear Nicola,

Thanks for the attached. We'll pass, I'm afraid. Autobiography dressed up as pop psychology isn't really our thing. I'm rather taken aback by the impression you have that I'm some grubby sexual predator. I have been in a stable relationship for more than five years now.

I told you that Hitchens anecdote in strictest CONFIDENCE. I wish you well with gaining the trust of another publisher — perhaps one interested in having casual sex with community leaders.

Best, Frank Hutcheson.

www.robinsonpublishing.eu

Social Capital, Social Interest: The Struggle For Social Mobility

© Nicola Murray 2009

Draft Preface

© Nicola Murray 2009

Politics is sometimes an argument, but it is always a conversation. And the politician's job, regardless of how important they are or which party they 'belong' to, is to have that conversation. To convince opponents, or the public, sometimes even one's own colleagues, of what one is saying, and to prove that point. It doesn't matter whether you are a nationally-recognised Secretary of State or an anonymous backbencher. We each of us have our voice and together in conversation those voices will be heard somewhere.

One of the things I have consistently argued against is the actually rather silly notion that politicians are somehow celebrities. We're not. Ours is a vocation, not simply some 'career choice'.

We are called into the spotlight. We do not seek the spotlight.

OK, maybe to some the combination of power and fame is a kind - perhaps a special kind - of celebrity. And for a worthy cause, be it Heart Awareness or be it Children In Need, I for one will climb aboard the famousness train. Yes, I admit, that was me 'singing' along with Bananarama for International Women's Day! Yes, guilty - that was me on the Moonwalk Against Breast Cancer with Janet Street-Porter and Lulu. Yes I confess, that WAS me attached to Ricky Gervais in the Comedylympics three-legged race!

Away from the glitz and glamour, however, a politician's life is all about hard work and dedication. About striving to build a better world for ordinary people. About justice. Fairness. Engagement. Enablement.

The one big personal passion that has driven me throughout my political career is social mobility. But what IS social mobility?

My dictionary defines 'social' as 'adj. relating to life in an organised community'. And 'mobility' as 'n. the quality or power of being mobile'. Life. Community. Power. In other words, the power of a community comes from the life within it. Or, even more significantly, the life of a community comes from the power within it. This power, this life, can remain trapped for generations. By poverty. By lack of ambition. By despair.

I believe there is tremendous untapped potential in communities throughout the country. My task as a politician is to help these communities discover the heroes within themselves. To empower. To energise. To inspire.

Oh the Naysayers, the cynics, will tell us that you can't create world class communities with words alone. That resources are needed, money etc. Well, I've got news for the Naysayers. A new world is coming. The times they are a-changin'. A new order is emerging. A climate of positivism.

Let us celebrate our communities. Enough of Naysaying. Let us instead have...Yaysaying!

Cynicism, aided in no small part by the media, permeates our culture. We need to change the perception. Change the game. Change our aspirations. We need communities that are viable, innovatively funded, with refurbished social infrastructure. In that process we can create a narrative that is heedless of sexual orientation, reaching new heights of excellence and coherence.

Each of the chapters in this personal overview of social mobility will address ways in which new positive thinking can be applied systematically and rigorously to the issues around it:

Skills and Education - more creative community opportunities for young people.

Competition and Intellectual Property – ideas for a Britain's Got Community-style knockout competition to find the country's most successful community, plus thoughts on social mobility set in the context of a national database.

Technology - more community-related issues on the internet, digitalisation, etc.

Business Support - more leaflets and a new cartoon character, e.g 'Hubbo', to nurture communities as a hub of social enterprise.

Diversity - more of EVERYTHING, to minimise barriers and stimulate innovation.

Infrastructure - more enablement for unique talents to blossom and to get from A to B.

Evidence - more demonstration of how this all works when joined up.

*

© Nicola Murray 2009

(Have to stop now – phew! What do you think Frank? x)

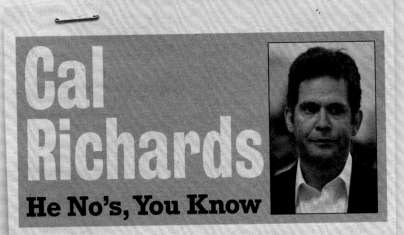

Cal Richards
He No's, You Know

Tasered for Being a Simple Englishman

SO, as a UK citizen theoretically still has a right to do, I intended to take a little walk down my street the other day. But as I stepped out of the front gate – BANG! I was tasered in the chest by an officious little s-d from the local council.

The last thing I saw as I hit the tarmac was his face looming over me like a black cloud. I awoke to find him beaming threateningly down with a toothy grin asking me 'If every 'ting was arright?'

And as I lay on the floor – thousands of volts coarsing through my quivering body – this 'pillar of the establishment', African naturally, at least so far as I could tell beneath his burka, stepped up and informed me he could not remove the electric prongs from my thorax, due to the need to have a female member of his team on hand, lest I later accused him of sexually molesting me!

'Just get the BLOODY THINGS OUT' I screamed, whereupon, he pepper-sprayed me full in the face – as he is apparently allowed to do under new EU noise abatement regulations monitored by our panoply of local speed cameras.

Of course, by the time his colleague chipped up on her peddle cycle, unable to speak a word of English, no doubt, despite the hundreds of thousands of pounds assuredly granted her to try to achieve this aim, I was practically soaked in my own ur*ne.

My crime? Apparently I had insufficiently sorted my recycling amongst the 39 different varieties of bin provided by the local eco-nazis. Now there used to be a little thing in this land known as habeus-corpus and a jolly fine little Anglo-Saxon by-law it was too! But now it seems to only apply to paedos and terrorists!

So after 48 hours of being indoctrinated in Guardian-approved words to use for fatties, rug munchers, chavs and our new Polish friends I was released blinking into the sunlight with my pants around my legs.

Sound like an exaggeration? Sound made-up? Well, as a matter of fact, it actually is. But it might not have been. And the fact that it could very well have been an actual TRUE STORY, correct in every detail had it not been invented by me, tells you all you need to know about The United StinK-ingdom after 13 years of misrule!

Stewart Pearson

SO, cuddly ad man 'Stew Pot' Pearson is helping Her Majesty's Loyal Opposition, such that it is, with its 'media strategy'. Well yippe dee do dah. Hang out the bunting. Mine's a Pimms and foccacia. With an ice cube made of cous cous.

Now as a man of the street I'm not exactly sure what a fancy-pants 'media strategy' is. Corrie at 6.30, Master-chefs at 9, that's my bli-kin' 'media strategy'.

He clearly watches neither — Coronation Street is on at 7.30, Masterchef at 8.00.

Part 4

Malcolm Tuckers's Guide To Journalism

Understanding Journalists

When dealing with hacks it's worth remembering at all times that they are shallow, venal, self-serving fuckpumps with a farcically inflated sense of their own importance. In other words, they are exactly like ministers. Though hacks typically drink more. And earlier in the day.

Crucially, journalists are less accountable and have even fewer moral convictions than a minister. Nobody – not even a minister – can ethically undercut a journalist. It is the only profession that actually produces a negative fucking score on the Scruple Index.

Like all ancient crafts and mysteries, journalism has its arcane laws. I'm about to tell you the secret, four-word First Rule Of Journalism. It is not, as you might be led to believe, some righteous mingefluff such as 'Seek After The Truth' or 'Defend Our Precious Freedoms'. It is 'Fill The Fucking Space'. The ultimate purpose of journalism is to plug a hole on the page with whatever arseplasma you can find. Understand this and you'll understand why we need fucking hacks to use our arseplasma, not theirs.

Journalism is like the ocean. There is a hierarchy, as there is in the world of fucking fish. Here is a rough key:

- Single-celled shit-dwelling local hacks
- Bottom-feeding regional correspondents
- Local radio coelocunths

- Tabloid jellyfucks
- Knobheaded broadsheet bloaters
- Basking cockless sharks [e.g Marr, Neil]
- The Dimbleby Whale
- Murdoch's Newstrawler, the Sky HD Pequod

News Reporters

Imagine the news process as a vast, pulsating digestive tract. Information is gobbled up at one end and eventually farted out the other. Collectively, news reporters form the lower intestine. Toxic gas erupts from time to time as 'breaking news'. It is a dark and constipated place. Summary: NEWS REPORTERS ARE ARSESHOLES WHO DON'T GIVE A SHIT.

You know the phrase 'you couldn't make it up'? Well, that phrase was made up by some hack fuck, astonished to find himself for once in possession of facts so fucking horrible they required no further embellishment. It rarely happens, which is why all news reports are called 'stories'.

News reporters are psychopaths. They're not looking for long-term fucking relationships with anyone. They just mug their victims, then move on to the next. They have no conscience. They feel no fucking compassion. They are never, never to be trusted.

A minister ambushed by these fucking weasels will wake up the following morning as a dislocated jumble of bruises, broken bones and lacerations, moaning softly underneath a snappy intro.

Feature Writers

News reporters regard themselves as technicians, assembling a story from the basic components of lies, topspin, hyperbole and fuckabout. Feature writers are artisans, crafting 2,000 words of contemplative 'story-telling' from guff, chuff, puff and fucking adverbs. Common themes are Where Did It All Go Wrong? and The Real Britain Today.

Feature writers are bleating, mimsy egomaniacs who specialise in long, empathetic lunches so they can wheedle out harmful personal details. Under no circumstances should a minister be allowed to talk to feature writers unaccompanied.

A minister interviewed solo by these oily jamrags will wake up the following morning as a slow-roasted fucking turkey with a fistful of sage and onion up their arse, served with a selection of embarrassing stories about their past life which somehow, after two bottles of claret and an armagnac, ended up ON THE FUCKING RECORD.

Columnists

Columnists are all vain wankers. Remember that in the world of journalism 'columnist' is sexual slang for 'someone fondling their own tiny little cockshaft while fisting themselves up the bugle'. A columnist is so far up himself he's punctured his kidneys. Of course, many columnists are women and don't technically have a cock. Just assume they're fondling their tiny little clits and have perforated their ovaries or fucking whatever with self-love .

We have limited influence over columnists, as they work in physical isolation from the rest of the world in an Edwardian house somewhere, with fucking cats and an Aga and Eva Cassidy on the fucking iPod. Columnists can dish it out but they can't take it. They are sensitive souls. Personal insults posted anonymously on the internet can wound, so ALWAYS fucking retaliate.

A minister who attracts the attention of a columnist will wake up the following morning crushed beneath a ponderous extended fucking metaphor.

Sketch Writers

Parliamentary sketch writers are basically 14-year-old public schoolboys who never got over their crush on Nanny. There are no women sketch writers. Why? Because the world of sketch writing is like a posh Gents in a five-star hotel. It smells of cologne and it's full of pissed cunts quipping in fucking French.

Sketch writers have a unique view of politics, looking down their fucking noses from the Press Gallery of the House of Commons and forming their eyebrows into Gothic fucking arches. The prissy shits. If a minister is under-briefed or performing weakly under questioning they might notice, if they're fucking awake. But they're mostly on the lookout for physical deformities, a funny voice etc so they can just fucking sneer.

A minister who draws down the effeminate ire of sketch writers will wake up the following morning to find themselves being compared to a character from fucking Dad's Army.

Cartoonists

How many times have you heard someone say "fuck, did you see that brilliant cartoon in the paper yesterday?" Exactly. Never. Cartoonists are just failed artists who couldn't draw the fucking curtains, never mind a proper caricature. They are driven by rage and self-loathing.

They're not much of a threat, but it's worth dropping a line to their editors from time to time complaining in general terms about racial stereotyping, sexism, political agenda etc to keep them on their fucking toes. If you meet one socially, be sure to point out any characteristics of enemy politicians they may have missed, e.g Peter Mannion looks like a fucking Friesian cow in a wig.

A minister who inspires a cartoonist will wake up the following morning to find themselves lampooned, with exaggerated features, spraying cartoon spittle and saying something shameful. Luckily nobody will recognise the minister, or understand what the fuck the cartoon's about, and will move straight on to the letters page.

Bloggers

Ugly word, ugly fucking people. Pale, bloated and flabby, they look like they've survived on a diet of KFC and biscuits in a cellar for the last 20 years. They haven't, of course. Nearly all of them are based in their fucking bedroom. In their Mum's house. They like to think of themselves as 'journalists', in the same way as those waddling cockstumps who wear a tabard saying Community Support Officer like to think of themselves as 'the police'.

Bloggers kid themselves that they are mavericks. Independent voices on the fringe, speaking up for the dispossessed. They are clinically fucking delusional. All they do is trade in gossip and rumour, like the teenagers in Costa Coffee they stare at, longingly. When bloggers claim that they can't be bought what they actually fucking mean is that they never get paid. For 'unbribeable' read 'unemployable'. They can usually be silenced by getting their internet service provider to run a trace on the sites they're visiting late at night.

A minister who crosses a blogger will wake up the following morning to find themselves at the centre of a shrill, un-spellchecked blizzard of misplaced apostrophes and very fucking poor grammar indeed.

How To Leak Stories

Scenario 1: Upfront and Personal

Sometimes the simplest solutions are the most effective. Let's say I meet a friendly hack, somewhere discreet. I tell them I've got something 'really juicy' and that I'm prepared to give them an exclusive first look at it. When they express interest, I tell them I've taken a fucking skipload of Cialis and now my cock's so engorged it needs to come out for air. Halfway through unzipping my trousers, I remove the look of frozen disbelief from their stupid fucking face by telling them I'm only kidding, I've got some inside information for them. They get a scoop. They keep it non-attributable. They owe me a favour. They apologise for believing even for a fucking MOMENT I would need Cialis for an engorged cock.

Scenario 2: The 'Accidental' Leak

Journalists have massive professional egos to feed. You can use this to con them into thinking they're doing their job properly for a fucking change by pretending to suppress something you want leaked. Call a press conference, say you know they've heard all sorts of rumours about The Story, and that a statement will be issued in due course. Take NO questions. Sweep out of the room and wait for the phone calls.

Or ring them up and insist on putting The Story into context. When they say they haven't heard about The Story, go quiet for 10 seconds. Make it sound like you're pissed off with yourself for having 'put it out there'. Then tell them The Story.

Or – and this is a personal fucking favourite of mine – intercept a minister on their way to Downing Street. Travel over with them in the car. Show them a sheet of A4 with The Story bulletpointed. Make sure it's on top of the pile of papers they're clutching when they arrive. Then just let them walk to the front door of Number 10, waving and smiling like a badly-sewn fucking hand puppet at the guys with the long lenses.

Scenario 3: The Reverse-Angle Fuck Leak

Not all the stories we want to leak are positive. Some of them are about the Opposition and are very fucking negative indeed. Obviously, you can use the non-attributable personal leak as described above.

Sometimes, though, when you REALLY want to launch a clusterfuck bomb up the enemy's unguarded rear, USE THE POWER OF LOCAL RADIO. Local radio HAS no fucking power, you say. Shut the fuck up, I say. That's my point. If you GIVE local radio some power you can be sure of some serious sphincter-splitting fuckery when the silly cunts DO use it.

Let me tell you about a little manoeuvre we pulled a few months ago. Oh, and I should say I'm telling you this in strict confidence. If this gets out I will blame each of you individually, track you down and punch your fucking faces into plasma.

We discovered a potentially embarrassing conflict of interest in the affairs of Lord Carville, the celebrated Opposition spokesman who's a very, very harsh critic of Her Majesty's Government. We knew Carville was appearing on a BBC Radio Cumbria phone-in to talk about his love of the countryside. Cumbria in particular. He fucking owns half of it.

So I got a certain special adviser – let's call him Oliver Reeder, working out of DoSAC – to ring up as 'Danny' with a question for Lord Carville. It went something like this: 'Lord Carville, you are critical of the government's rural development policy. You stress your own party's commitment to the conservation of our countryside. How do you reconcile this with being a major shareholder in FG Properties, a development company registered in Belize, which is about to submit an outline planning application for 237 starter homes, a supermarket and all necessary infrastructure in an area of outstanding natural beauty 15 miles west of Cirencester?'

That's quite a long question Danny, the producer says. I could text it over, says Danny. Or send a hard copy. I'm getting 'number unavailable' on my screen here, she says . Can I ask where you're ringing from, Danny? So Danny says if I tell you something in confidence, can I be absolutely certain it will go no further? I actually work for Lord Carville, in a public relations capacity. The thing is, sooner or later this story about him being a conservationist in public and a property developer in private is going to get out. People will say he's been concealing his business interests.

By now the producer's intrigued. But Danny's got another trick up his sleeve. Yeah, he says, so we thought if we planted a question about it on Radio Cumbria – which no offence is probably being listened to right now by one farmer and a fucking sheep with a broken leg – we could later demonstrate full transparency in the public domain.

Obviously the producer has taken full metal umbrage but she knows she's sitting on a big story. Danny says remember Lord Carville's expecting this question. He's great at looking surprised and ambushed, so just play along. He may even threaten to walk out. He's really good. The producer says has she got this right: Carville wants to use her phone-in as a way of legitimising his own commercial activities?

Danny says yeah, that's it in a nutshell. What's your email? I'll send over the background on this, make the questions look informed. I don't want to sound patronising but I'm guessing any 'researcher' there is some squint-eyed fat fuck retard foisted on you by a local social services placement scheme.

End of call. We nudge a couple of hacks in the right direction, but by the following morning news of Carville's secret property empire's all over the wires anyway. He's blustering about being sabotaged by an impostor but who's fucking listening to HIM now?

We could have trickled the story out in a conventional way. But this caused much more damage. Local radio had a scoop, the national hacks were thrashing round in a fucking fisting frenzy, Lord Carville was forced to quit frontline politics and I got to find out what it's like standing over someone with a steak tenderiser while they read out your script.

Destroy this document. My lovely assistant Sam will contact you shortly to make sure you have. If you haven't, destroy yourself. Please let me know if you require any fucking assistance with this.

How To Bury Bad News

Sam—
Please distribute this to the usual fuckspads.
Cheers, M

Scenario 1: The Fucktastrophe

I don't need to tell you the origin of the phrase 'bury bad news'. Do I? We all learned some hard lessons from 9/11. The real tragedy there was twofold: the heartbreaking fucking stupidity of actually sending the 'bury bad news' email in the first place, and then not successfully burying THAT fucking story when it subsequently broke.

 Of course, nobody wants an appalling disaster that kills loads of people just so it becomes a major story and eclipses everything else, including your shitty little press release about a £50m overspend on computer procurement. Nobody. However, if you CAN delay the announcement of bad news, it might be worth waiting for the following stories to break:

- North Korea launches a successful 'gay bomb' attack on Indonesia.
- The Prince of Wales goes on I'm A Celebrity, Get Me Out Of Here, talks in his fucking Goon voices all the time and keeps pissing the campfire out.
- Lady Gaga suddenly appears on the Moon, having sex with a robot dog.
- Israel apologises for something.
- All the spectators at a Newcastle United home match go up in a fucking blaze of fat and sugar.
- Extraterrestrial creatures land on top of the United Nations building and do a wriggly dance.
- A cure for cancer is officially announced by scientists on a new game-changing, mould-breaking, envelope-pushing chat show featuring Charlie Fucking Brooker in a dress.
- Sting and McCartney die in a horrific double murder involving a Hofner bass guitar, bagpipes and a fucking lute.

In other words, don't hold your fucking breath you moron.

Scenario 2: The 'Fog You'

Assuming there is no convenient international breaking news story to obliterate your fuck-up, make the information imfuckingpenetrafuckingble. Let's take that procurement example, as it's real. Though of course nobody knows that, do they?

Make the press release NOT about how some speccy mungo in Communications spunked £50m of taxpayers' money on some faff that's turned out to be as essential a 'networking tool' as a fucking Amstrad E-mailer. No. Instead, drag that silly cunt out of Communications, shout at him until he cries, then physically pin him to a fucking chair and poke him with something until he types out four paragraphs of complete bullshit about 'beta systems' and 'future savings of around £1 billion a year expected from smartcloud delivery' etc with lots of technical gash so tangled nobody will ever bother to unpick it.

Say.

Scenario 3: The Slip It In Quietly, Vicar

If your arse-biting news has been announced on a hidden page of the Department's website where it can only be found by accident, so fucking what? It's still been announced, hasn't it? It's not your fault. If it's anyone's fault, my money would be on a certain snivelling quimfart from Communications. You may detect a theme emerging here.

"Oh fuck" you say. "Apologies, ladies and gentlemen of the press. There was no attempt to conceal this information – indeed, the Department is PROUD to have brought this project in on time and only slightly over budget. It was a genuine human error..."

Once the human fucking error has been identified, given ownership of the fuck-up, then dangled before a stave-wielding press like the mute piñata of fucking blame he is, he can be sacked.

Scenario 4: The Super-Injunction

Stay tuned on this one. I'm currently exploring – with the legendary Posh Ronald from Legal – the possibility of exploiting a loophole. Now I could make a joke about exploiting your loophole at this point, but it would fucking demean both of us and distract us from the issue here. Which is that this is strictly, and I mean very fucking strictly to the point where we need a safe word to avoid accidental death strictly, confidential.

It is possible, theoretically, under certain circumstances, to suppress information we don't want in the public realm by triangulating the story to include a third party. As almost every Government initiative is contracted at some level to private sector consultants, there may be a way of gagging the press with a super-injunction if we offer the consultants an incentive, i.e do as we fucking say or that's the last contract you get from us, you perfumed cunts.

We would need a very hostile team of solicitors – and by hostile I mean friendly - to represent our consultants and to argue that the story here was so sensitive the press were not allowed to report it, or to refer to the injunction. Of course, it may seem fucking nuts, a Government effectively taking out an injunction against itself to prevent itself from announcing something it doesn't want to say. But that's the law for you. Possibly.

There is, of course, my own Need To Know gagging order on this document. I'm sure I don't need to remind you how diligently I will pursue this, with fucking duct tape. And with my gagging orders there ARE no fucking safe words.

Best regards,

Malcolm Tucker

Malcy,

Sir Trevor Fridge-Magnet or whoever the gelded fuck is who used to run Mothercare, got this letter of Julius' from a friend in the City. He sent it over to me with a 'thanks' for all the accelerated planning applications. Thought you might like it to stick in your wee book of Panini stickers entitled 'My Big Fat Fucking Folder Full of Nicholson Filth, Folie-de-Grandeur and Foolhardy Attempts to come over as Some Sort of Fully Functioning Human Fucking Being and not a Follicley Challenged Fop With a Face like a Fart Cushion and a Fucking Cheek Bigger than Mount Fuji'.

Yes We're Cunts. J x

London SW1

April 19th 2010

Dear Jeremy

The game's afoot, man the lifeboats, take to the hills, it's a wolf, don't panic, I am Spartacus, no, I am Spartacus, cry God for Harry, do not go gentle into that good night, Schnell! Schnell! Achtung! Schnell!! etc. My point is, we're buggered, and pretty soon the electorate will tell us so. Personally I think a hard and feisty rogering from the populace is what this crew of carcasses needs. There are one or two decent eggs under whom it has been a pleasure to roll out delivery, but frankly the general spread of talent has been trickier to spot than a Higgs Boson.

I tell you, Jeremy, there have been things that have taken place inside Number 10 that would make your mother turn. I've seen grown women pulped into compote and intelligent men, All Souls material on a good day, reduced to the status of children's entertainers. Not v. inspiring.

That said, as I put on my civvies, I wonder if my experiences and network of very good associates can be of use to you or your Board of Directors? I have built up a thorough working knowledge of governmental process-points, have actioned a terrific medley of inter-departmental initiatives (the Clean Hospital-Staff Act was my handiwork) and my roller deck of contacts is a beacon of excellence. In short, I know where the bodies are buried, I know who buried them, what they used, how they cleaned up after, where they buried those implements in turn, and what are the long-term consequences for the soil in that area. See me as, in effect, an industrio-economic Miss Marple, ready to do your bidding, solving any crimes (i.e., getting the right people into a meeting and bashing a few heads together until we can come up with an effective IT/infrastructure/private-public-partnership solution) and then calling in the police (i.e., presenting a fully-bound report to your Board of Directors).

Needless to say, I'd merit top whack for this kind of service, but I can assure you, for the money I will guarantee you a man who is sharp, focused, lean, hungry, and, above all, proactive.

Do let me know your thoughts and, in the meantime, much love to your family and such.

Best

[signature]

Lord Nicholson

Jamie, as soon as the sick baldsack steps out of Number 10 for the last time, you have my permission to take him out with any type of long range weapon. But do me a favour; use that long range weapon at very very close range.

Love and fucks, M. x

To : Malcolm Tucker [mailto: dontblamemenowthateverythingisfucked@gmail.com]
From : Stuart Edridge – Head of Entertainment [mailto: sedridge@bbc.co.uk]
Subject : You
Attachments : Malcolm proposal.doc

Chat Show Correspondence

Hi Malcolm,

Sorry to intrude on your inbox unannounced (if you'll pardon the expression) – I got your email from Sam who said it'd be cool to get in touch.

First of all, can I say how fucking sorry I am that your lot are out. Obviously, I'm not saying this with my BBC hat on. (We don't have hats now anyway. Cutbacks.) But I was totally rootin' for you bro. I really thought you were going to turn it around with a late winner – a Steven Gerrard style screamer into the top corner! And if anyone could have done it it's you - and I'm not just saying that because I'm trying to be your bum chum. Although obviously I would give myself up to you for gay sex even though I am married with twins (children not wives.) (Sadly.) (Twin wives would be awesome.)

Anyway, after I got over the shock of what the country had done - 'Bad country! In your bed!' - it got me thinking. Our nation's disastrous loss could be my gain. You're suddenly unemployed and that is just plain wrong because, IMHO, you are THE greatest performer this country has right now. Apologies again for sounding like I want to give you a blowy round the back of TV Centre but seriously the way you OBLITERATED everyone on the Election Night coverage was A-mazing. You're on fire right now. No one on British TV could touch that – not Simon Cowell, not Caroline Quentin, not even Michael McIntyre. You're a powerhouse. (Stay with me – I promise I'm not about to tell you I'm in love with you. Although, obviously, I am a little bit in love with you.) You're like a (very, very) white Richard Pryor. You have a righteous indignation. Not the crap fake indignation that Jeremy Clarkson does where he whinges on about his ipod earphones getting in a tangle like a whiney bitch. You, sir, are the real fucking deal.

Now it may be that you're inundated with offers – wouldn't surprise me. You've probably already been asked to write your memoirs. Maybe Peter Morgan will do a Frost/ Nixon style play about you. He bloody should do! (Actually that's not a bad idea. I'm going to forward this to Ben over in Drama. I think that could be really exciting.) But – I thought I'd take a chance and get in touch anyway. Fuck it – it's a massive long shot I know but if you don't ask you don't get, right? Not unless you're a Catholic priest.

So, here I am asking.

Would you be interested in hosting a chat show for us?

Or, fuck it, anything else you'd be interested in doing for that matter.

I have to say I'm particularly psyched about the idea of you doing a chat show though. I'm thinking something that's a cross between Question Time and Graham Norton. Smart, funny, irreverent. With a mix of guests from intellectual big hitters to big name celebrities. I don't know – Stephen Fry, Obama and Katie Price. Not that, but you get the idea. Although that sounds pretty fucking sexy to me!

And there's you as host – angrily grilling them within an inch of their lives, like Paxman on crystal meth being given a wedgie by Matthew Wright. If that makes sense. I'm not sure it even does – that's how excited I am. I've lost the ability to form coherent sentences.

I know one of my colleagues talked to you about doing a show called Through The Shit which you passed on. (It's going ahead with loveable non-rapist Jack Tweed as host. Although if you did decide you were interested we could drop him.) But I see this as something completely different and totally fucking fresh.

We'd record the show rather than put it out live. The idea being to give you as much freedom as possible to do and say whatever you like. Obviously, we may have to bleep bits here and there and the lawyers will edit some stuff out for their bullshit legal reasons but basically you can go crazy. By pre-recording the show we can give you the licence to be as raw and edgy and close to the bone as you can be. Then we can always cut it later.

I genuinely think this could be the best show on TV ever. I'd watch it and I hate TV! I smell Baftas. Seriously. This stinks of Bafta.

It's obviously not One. But it could go late night BBC Two. Or even on Three if we skewed it more to the kids. That would mean less political heavyweights and more guests like Peaches Geldof / Ralf Little / Danny Dyer – but how tasty would that be?

I realise you're busy (perhaps not as busy as you were last week!) but have a think.

I've attached a rough outline. It's just a discussion document but hopefully it'll get the creative juices flowing!

b,
S

From : Malcolm Tucker [mailto: dontblamemenowthateverythingisfucked@gmail.com]
To : Stuart Edridge – Head of Factual Entertainment [mailto: sedridge@bbc.co.uk]
Subject : RE : You

Hi Stuart,

Thanks for your email, mate.

I've mulled it over and here's my take on it :

It's a great offer. It really is. And I'd love to take it but there's one slight drawback in that I'd rather cut off my own bollocks and sell them to Waitrose as hairy Scotch eggs.

1. The first problem with a chat show is this : it would involve me talking to people. I fucking hate people. People are cunts.

Now you might say to that, 'Really? Do you really think that? Or is that some kind of intellectual posturing designed to shock'. To which I would answer, 'No, I really think that. People are cunts. Have you met people? I have. And the people I've met have all been massive cunts'.

2. The second problem with my having a chat show is it would involve me being a chat show host. And the problem with chat show hosts is that they're all cunts. I – and this is counter-intuitive but bear with me – am not a cunt.

3. The third problem is that you are asking me and although I've never met you I think we can both agree that you are a cunt.

4. I don't want to question your expertise on this subject – I know you were the guys who gave Davina McCall and Lily Allen their own chat shows and obviously they were roaring successes and you know what you're doing – but shouldn't you be asking someone with a proven track record of being a chat show host / cunt. I don't know, someone like Piers Morgan, for example.

5. In the recent election your 'organisation' basically sided with the in-bred opposition because you were scared if you didn't – if you just stayed fucking neutral – they'd accuse you of bias. So your offer is a bit like Nazi sympathisers at the end of the war asking Churchill if he wanted to put on a cheeky cabaret. To which I think he might have responded something like, 'Never. You cunts'.

So, overall, I think it's a no. But thanks for getting in touch and do bear me in mind for other projects.

Enormous retards,

Malcolm xxx

MALCOLM TUCKER TALKS THE TALK

(WORKING TITLE)

Spin supremo Malcolm Tucker sticks his hand down the throat of celebrity and rips out its innermost secrets and maybe some organs and mucus and stuff.

Malcolm Tucker steps out of the shadows and into the limelight and goes from Spinmeister to Chatmeister.

POSSIBLE OPENING CREDITS SEQUENCE :

Malcolm walks out of Number Ten on his way to TV Centre. His face is like thunder. On the way he gets stopped by a chugger – he punches her in the face. He passes London Zoo and gets attacked by a lion – he kills it with his bare hands. He walks past the Iranian embassy which is under siege again. He grabs a machine gun off a Bobby and mows down the bad guys in balaclavas. He arrives at TV Centre. Looks in a mirror, slightly adjusts his tie and walks into the studio with a big smile.

Malcolm walks on to the set. It has a whiff of Westminster intrigue but it's funky and bright and accessible.

Malcolm does a vicious but hilarious monologue about what's happening in the world this week.

Then he introduces his house band. Four Poofs And A Piano are out.

Ladies and Gentlemen, please welcome … The Honourable Members.

Malcolm does some edgy but funny stuff about their name, etc.

And then it's time to crack on with the show. And what a show we have for you tonight. It will rock your world. Please welcome …

These are just some ideas don't take them as gospel …
(I've divided them into groups. Famous Scots. Political figures. People I'd like to see you give a bollocking to. Women. And general all round good chat show guests.)

ALL ROUND GOOD CHAT SHOW GUESTS:

Stephen Fry, Obama, Katie Price, Ricky Gervais, Kim Cattrall, Danny Dyer, Megan Fox, Prince Charles, a Dalek, Woody Allen, Oprah.

FAMOUS SCOTS:

Sean Connery, Billy Connolly, Kelly MacDonald

POLITICAL FIGURES:

(Obama) I'm open to suggestions on this one – SE.

PEOPLE I'D LIKE TO SEE YOU GIVE A BOLLOCKING TO:

Paris Hilton, Russell Crowe, Tiger Woods, Adrian Chiles, Jeremy Clarkson, Kay Burley, the murderer Charles Bronson (we could do a video link with Charles Bronson in prison. Imagine that!)

OTHER POSSIBLE TITLES FOR THE SHOW:

Tucker's Tongue Lashing

Malcolm in the Middle. (Set/seating arrangement would have to reflect this.)

Tough Talk with Malcolm Tucker

Tucked In. (The interviews are done in bed. Could be funny!)

IDEAS FOR OTHER SHOWS :

Malcolm Tucker Investigates … Tourettes.

Tucker's Luck (A sideways look at the world of gambling.)

Malcolm Tucker's Spin The Bottle (Idea for a gameshow. Don't know what it would be yet – just have the title.)

From : Malcolm Tucker [mailto : mtucker@gov.org.uk]
To: Michael Oswalt [mailto : Michael.Oswalt@thenewstatesman.co.uk]
Subject : Book Reviews

Book Reviews

Hey Mike – can you wait till after the National Executive votes – if I manage to get my goons to spike Dan Miller's cock print the second one, if he's still a swinging dick go for the first which crawls up his arse so that I may infiltrate his digestive tract and better strangulate him later. Cheers mate. MT

A New Beginning: By Dan Miller
Review by Malcolm Tucker

In the wake of his successful rise within the party it is timely that we should be gifted this new collection of Miller's pieces written for Prospect over the last 12 years. This tightly written collection of clear-eyed think-pieces on the state of the nation provides perhaps the closest thing to a road-map the centre-left possesses at this time of national renewal. Miller has long been one to watch but with these essays he establishes himself as more than a brilliant and charismatic young politician, he is also a heavyweight of political thought. Long may he prosper!

Or

A New Beginning: By Dan Miller
*Review by Malcolm Tucke*r

After his recent humiliation in the party's leadership elections it is something of a surprise to see this little collection of damp squibs struggle into print. Grubbing around in his bottom drawer, man-molehill Miller has clearly decided a fast buck might be accrued by stapling together this random scrote-bag of 'articles' and souped up restaurant reviews. Why on earth he thinks we should be interested in such matters as the changing menu at his local gastro pub and what it says about 'Englishness' I have no idea. But I do know that the party he claims to love has done the right thing in sending this poor man's Tony Crosland to the reclamation site of history. Good riddance!

Saturday Review

POLITICS
Reviewed by **Malcolm Tucker**

Ben Swain: Britain: It Ain't Broken

Ben Swain's stellar career lit up the political firmament like a firework a few years back. It shimmered with promise as it ascended to a mighty apex before giving out a phut of disappointing proportions and falling back to the ground to be pored over by primary school children who pulled apart the metaphorical casing to peer in at the blackened, empty, burnt-up workings beneath.

Swain has latterly been vituperative in his comments about the 'spin doctors' who worked for his party during this time in the sun. It is perhaps ironic he should now so loudly rail against the influence of the 'image makers', as when he first walked into my office he was perhaps the most eager and certainly the largest and most unsightly turd to ever seek my bespoke polishing services.

In any case this reprint of his 2007 meditation on the nature of social change in a multi-polar post-market-capitalist world makes essential reading for anyone who has wondered what it is like to be in a persistent vegetative state but doesn't want to go to the trouble of actually suffering a head on collision with a horse chestnut tree.

Cheers for writing these up for me Ollie. Please accept this practically untouched bottle of blended supermarket scotch whiskey as a token and indeed a full expression of my thanks. You really are a mean spirited little shit house aren't you? They're just lovely. Many thanks! MT

Cliff Lawton: Time At The Top

Like a much awaited package of 1980s caravan catalogues Cliff Lawton's recollections of his period as a cabinet minister thudded onto my desk last week with the sort of thwack I generally associate with the arrival of a mid-sized bag of potting compost.

As this 840 page magnus opus (by my reckoning 210 pages per year in government) tested the soundness of the lower back of the postal worker who delivered it, I pondered who would be reading this piece of reportage culled from Mr Lawton's time inhabiting the stratospheric heights of the now revamped Department for Social Affairs?

As I settled down with a selection of over-the-counter stimulants and tried for the third time to make it through the prologue I thumbed nervously through a number of the forthcoming sections: 'First Steps' (covering in a less than brisk 40 pages the time up to his graduation from nursery school), 'Political Re-education' (ensuring he generously mentions by name everyone he met at Durham University from 1974 to 1977) and 'At the Summit!' (this initial summit being the office of constituency secretary for the Cumberland Labour Party, the first of a large number of peaks, summits and mountaintops scaled by the political mountaineer Lawton).

The media seems understandably to have latched on to the one paragraph in the book that is not laced with Lawton's trademark brand of literary Mogadon. It recounts how, by his version, Cliff, 'maintained my dignity as I was bundled out of office like so many carrots or pigs at a county fair by political svengali Malcolm Tucker'.

Rather than 'walking out' on a Government 'corrupt on the drunkenness of its own reckless stupidity and no longer worthy of the service of serious centre-left intellectuals' I seem to recall Lawton begging to be given any post, 'even Paddy-wrangling at Stormont or some bullshit in Europe', and looking for all the world like he would deliver oral pleasure to anyone who might let him be the boss of something.

Obviously for legal reasons I am unable to comment on his claims about what happened that day in the corridors at Social Affairs, but suffice to say that I have never seen an office stapler with jaws wide enough to do what is alleged.

Since leaving office under something of a cloud Cliff has remodelled himself as a self -styled 'voice of conscience' within the party. I can only say that his legs must be extremely wide to straddle the twin horses of radical political freethinking and his work on behalf of British Nuclear Fuels, British Petroleum, Kuwait National Holdings and the manufacturer of a certain brand of electronic cattle prod who does not in any way endorse the use of their technology in the many nations with repressive regimes to whom they export which appear to have no domestic dairy herds.

Overall 'Time At The Top' achieves one remarkable feat – despite being one of the most skull creakingly dull pieces of political autobiography to emerge in the modern era (and I include within this estimation the works of John Selwyn Gummer) it still never quite manages to capture the feeling of depression one felt when sharing a room with Cliff Lawton.

To: Whom It May Concern, My Successor

From: Nicola Murray,
        Secretary of State for Social Affairs and Citizenship*

Congratulations! As you have opened the envelope marked 'FAO: The new Secretary of State for Social Affairs and Citizenship' I assume you are now making yourself very much at home here.

It is a giddy thought, to think that as I sit here staring around this empty office after everyone has gone home, and thinking that this may be the last time I will ever see it, that at the same time someone else i.e you, in the future, is sitting exactly where I am and looking around at the same office and thinking 'so this is my office'. Perhaps I am 'overthinking', one of my trademark Nicola Murray faults, but then I have always firmly believed that 'overthinking' is preferable to 'underthinking'!

Anyway, this might seem an 'afterthought' to you but it is very much 'forward thinking' for me! This may sound like a joke, but it is not.

For, although you have an advantage over me in that you (obviously) know the result of the General Election and it hasn't happened for me yet, I have the advantage over you in having occupied your chair ('our chair'? sounds a bit odd, doesn't it?) before you. I would like to offer you, if I may, some perspective and advice.

Wow. This is like one of those science fiction stories, where the character gets a message from the future, isn't it, except this of course is a message from the past. For you, I mean. Obviously, it is written in the present for me. (Oh-oh. Overthinking again. Nicola Murray ™!)

You'll have met Terri and Robyn by now, of course. And I am sure they'll have tried, in their own way, to 'show you the ropes'. My advice is, 'Don't get caught in the rigging'. You will have plenty of time to learn the mysteries of civil service protocol. That can wait. Just shoo them out of 'our office' (actually, that does sound OK after all). Take off your shoes. 'Chill out' for half an hour. Decompress. Politics, as we both know, is a stressful business at the best of times. Believe me, there will be occasions in the not too distant future when you'll yearn for this quiet moment of bliss.

Yes, if there's one thing I learned fairly early on, it is that there is the world of politics 'out there' and the parallel world of politics 'in here'.

The world of politics 'in here' is in many ways more demanding. You are not just The Boss to the DoSAC community/family, you are a role model, almost a spiritual leader, if that doesn't sound too corny or pretentious. By all means 'be their friend' but 'be their friend' at a slight distance. It avoids all sorts of unpleasantness.

Well, I should really be on my way. The hustings beckon! Perhaps my party will stay in government and I will be back where you (we!) are sitting now. In which case, you won't be reading this at all. Unless – dread thought – you are on MY side and have REPLACED ME as Secretary of State for Social Affairs and Citizenship.**

Good luck. And I hope you're not reading this! (oh dear, yet MORE Nicola Murray Overthinking™!)

Best regards,

Nicola Murray

Nicola Murray

*NB at time of writing

** In which case, and please, PLEASE ignore if you're NOT a party colleague, FUCK YOU. (I'm joking) (I'm actually not).

EYE NEED

SENIOR FIGURE SEEKS HIP YOUNG GUNSLINGER TO COLLABORATE ON LITERARY MASTERWORK. I will talk. You will listen – go away and type. Influences include: A. Trollope, E. Waugh, J. J. Joyce, Herodotus, Gramsci, Freud, R. Ludlum & R. Hargreaves. Reply to PO Box Number. Confidentiality agreement must be signed. Or cock/tits detached and left as hostage.

EYE BUSINESS

Dear 'M'

Please find attached the first page or so as discussed. See what you think. I'm pretty pleased.

Thank you for the shisha pipe and all the chewing grass. I'd never been to that part of London before, what an interesting place to meet! (Would you even say it was London, there?) Hopefully you'll be more relaxed next time. And I think you can relax, I'm not sure you're as famous as you think you are! What are you though? Ex-central defender for Falkirk was my best guess, although I'm sure I'm miles out!

Best to you.

Robbie

Robbie Uppingham

TICKER TIME

Chapter 1

The tough psychoanalyst Mike Ticker took one look at the Prime Minister. He looked the big fucker in the eye.

'I know you pretty well PM.'
'Pretty fucking well, Mike.'
'Damn right. And I know when's something's bugging you. It used to be poverty. But you're on that now, you're all over it. Then it was the power industry but you soon deregulated those particular bastards. What is it PM, what's up?'
'Well Mike, I guess I've got to know you pretty well too. So I don't mind telling you. It's the nuclear codes Mike. They're gone. I've fucking lost them.'
'Fuck,' exhaled Mike.
'Exactly,' chipped in the PM.
'And no one knows apart from you. I've told you now. So you know. But you're the only one. I can trust you Mike. I can't trust the others. Only you. What am I going to do?'

Tucker took in the pleading eyes of the PM. He scanned the room. He wasn't one for mucking about. Ever. His big brain made the decision in superfast time and before he knew it his lips were saying the words he knew they were going to say:

'There's a back way out of here PM. Let's fucking roll!'

And with that Mike searched the back of his safe for his old service automatic and a packet of bullets. Nice. He was back in the shit. And the shit felt good.

This is all fine, up to a point. Not as good as what I said, but it'll do. I reckon it needs something arty up top. Something about a cloud? Clouds look like — butter? or sheep? "The clouds that morning looked like buttery sheep and Mike had a bone-on like a yew tree. By the time he rolled into work the sky was the colour of guns and the rain lashed him in the face like a piss, etc..." Not exactly this but a bit more atmosphere — for the reviewers — at the very start. MT.

Chapter 2

Mike grabbed the first anti-war protester by the scruff of his head.

'Where are the codes, garbage bag?' Mike said as he shook him none too nicely.

'I'll never tell you, Mike Warhead!' replied the grimy shithouse out of the corner of his tattooed mouth.

'I think you fucking will,' said Mike cracking one of the protestor's finger bones with a smash.

Finger bones pop when you break them, not smash. Just so you know. MT

and switching on the electric drill with a flick.

'No. You and your PM took this country to war, and if we have to blow this whole country up to get you back then that's just what we'll love to do!' said the mangled drug-head.

Mike revved the Bosch with relish.

'Where would you like it sonny? Up the cock hole or down the anus, cos one way or another, you're talking to me!'

We need to feel Mike's pain here more. He should drill the druggie with regret. With a noble sadness for the greater good of the people. Remember, later on we're going to find out the drug head was working for the CIA and Mike has his Hour of Darkness. MT.

From : MT [mailto : mt127@hotmail.co.uk]
To : Robbie Uppingham [mailto : RobbieU@googlemail.co.uk]
Subject:

Robbie you're fired. I've read this all back sober and it's fucking pish. You never wrote as good as I talked.

Goodbye, forever.
M

TRANSCRIPT *of telephone call 09.07.06, connection logged
at 02:26. Number 10, outgoing [handset C1] caller MALCOLM
TUCKER, Director of Communications. Recipient, home
landline, DAVID FANNING, minister for schools.*

DF   Malcolm. What the fuck? It's...it's half past two in
        the fucking morning.

MT   Oh boo hoo, pisshead. Unless you've rigged up some
        kind of fucking intravenous brandy shunt, I'm guessing
        you're not technically drinking right now.

DF   I'm not an alcoholic, Malcolm.

MT   *[inaudible]* And it's about five hours before you have
        the first of your fucking breakfast Screwdrivers. So
        maybe now, at *[inaudible]* 2.27 a.m, there's a chance
        we can get through a conversation without you spilling
        something on your fucking pyjamas or bursting into
        tears.

DF   This had better be an emergency Malcolm. I have a very
        busy day tomorrow.

MT   Oh yeah, let me help you with that. I think we might
        be able to significantly reduce your fucking workload.

DF   No.

MT   Give you the opportunity to spend more time with your
        hangover.

DF   No.

MT   I'm afraid yes, Dave. Consider your improvised
        comedy cabaret last night as a farewell performance.
        Blundering around a dinner dance like some pissed
        football mascot, you *[inaudible, volume distortion,
        possibly 'cumstain']*?

DF   Malcolm. It was a party for Christ's sake, not a
        fucking funeral.

MT   Your funeral, pal. Your funeral. There's been an
        official complaint. President of the fucking National
        Association of Head Teachers says you verbally
        assaulted her.

DF   That's bullshit.

10 DOWNING STREET
LONDON SW1A 2AA

MT   Then you felt her tits.

DF   No.

MT   Bit of a blurry, slurry fucking blank, is it?

DF   I can't fucking remember it because it didn't fucking
      happen. I'm not an alcoholic.

MT   Dave, that's exactly what I've been telling
      journalists for weeks. He's not an alcoholic. He was
      on painkillers. It was a loose bit of carpet. He was
      having a fucking diabetic hypo. All those times, I
      said you weren't an acoholic. And you weren't, right?

DF   I...

MT   And now I'm saying that last night you WERE an
      alcoholic. Up to you. Either I was wrong then or I'm
      wrong now. Either way you're dead in a pool of your
      own piss.

DF   How fucking dare you, actually, Malcolm. My
      drinking...

MT   Oh, I don't give a pig's wank about your drinking,
      Dave. We're heaving your fat arse out of the balloon
      because you're fucking useless. That Select Committee
      appearance. We could have pushed a fucking walrus
      into a cheap suit and sat it in front of the fucking
      microphone. You're shit. You're beyond shit. You're
      metashit. You're ultrashit.

DF   This is outrageous. So you're saying I'm sacked but
      that my drink...issues have nothing to do with it?

MT   Would you like them to have something to do with it?
      As I say, I can brief either way. 'He wanted to say
      goodbye personally, but it's after lunch, so he's in
      the Gents being doubly incontinent and puking, like
      the gurgling middle-aged fucking baby he is'. You
      [inaudible, volume distortion, possibly 'cockbun']

      [terminated by caller]

****

10 DOWNING STREET
LONDON SW1A 2AA

TRANSCRIPT of telephone call 12.04.05, connection logged
at 09:13. Number 10, outgoing [handset C4] caller MALCOLM
TUCKER, Director of Communications. Landline recipient
DARAGH SMITHSON, journalist.

DS   Hello.

MT   Daragh. Malcolm Tucker.

DS   Oh.

MT   How are things at the Telegraph? Must be feet up on
the fucking desk. No room for your political insight,
is there? Now your august fucking organ of record
fills up its pages with photos of the Harry Potter
girl touching herself. Or upskirt shots of Dr Who's
companion in a St Trinian's uniform.

DS   What do you want, Malcolm?

MT   Nothing mate. Just thought I'd ring for a catch-up.
Social call.

DS   Right. Fuck you. I'm recording this conversation.

[recipient handset recorder activated]

MT   Whoa whoa whoa. There's no need to be like that, is
there? Honestly mate, if you're busy...

DS   *[inaudible]*

MT   Hey, no problem. I'll give you a bell some time, yeah?

DS   Sure. I...

MT   Oh, by the way. Lewis sends his regards.

DS   Lewis?

MT   Yeah, you know. Big bloke? West Country accent?

[recipient handset recorder de-activated]

MT   Drug dealer? Asked me to send his regards. I've got a
note here. Says "Please tell Daragh Smithson I hope he
enjoyed the 3.5 grams of cocaine I supplied him with
on Tuesday April 10 at the Crown public house..."

DS   Malcolm. *[inaudible]* What the fuck?

MT Daragh? Can't hear you. You'll have to speak up.

DS I'm...interested to hear that. Please, go on.

MT Ah, sorry. Forgot. People around you. OK. I'll talk.
You listen, yeah? You naughty, naughty Class A
fuckbag.

DS *[inaudible]*

MT Yeah. See, someone - an anonymous someone with really
fucking excellent contacts in the media - heard this
rumour that a certain Sunday wankrag was planning to
sell coke to the son of a certain Home Office minister.
And film it.

DS Really. I did not know that.

MT Mm. So somehow - and I have to say the details are
very, very fucking vague - a certain public-spirited
dealer, let's call him West Country Lewis, was
encouraged to take the initiative.

DS Oh God. Mm. I see.

MT So Lewis made discreet enquiries to every single
newsdesk of every national newspaper. Told them he
knew that this son of a certain Home Office minister
was a user. That he knew the pub he frequented. That
he was pretty sure with the right sort of financial
incentive he could set up a sting. Then the journo
could tip off the police and fucking bingo.

DS Shit. Shit shit shit. Shit.

MT Well, obviously some newsdesks would have nothing to
do with it. But still, you'll never guess how many
hacks took West Country Lewis aside and asked him if
they could score some coke. Privately, for themselves.
Amazing, really, when you think how many of these
hypocritical fucking *[inaudible, volume distortion,
possibly 'cock stumps']* were prepared to write shocked
pieces about the minister's son. I say "you'll never
guess". It doesn't matter. I've got a fucking list.

DS What...how do you see this going forward?

MT Not sure yet. Thought I'd sound you out. You and all
the other sad, chang-snorting shit-for-brains hack
fuckers. Welcome your thoughts. And your cooperation.
Oh, got to go. Lobby briefing.

10 DOWNING STREET
LONDON SW1A 2AA

DS Wait.

MT I'll be in touch. Oh, and Daragh?

DS Yeah.

MT I really fucking admire you. You've got a really good
    nose for news. Dozy cunt.

    [terminated by caller]

****

TRANSCRIPT *of telephone call 15.01.09 connection logged
at 19:55. Number 10, outgoing [handset C1] caller MALCOLM
TUCKER, Director of Communications. Landline recipient:
DONALD MINCHIN MEP for Mercia South. Receiving handset in
conference mode.*

DM Hello.

MT Malcolm Tucker.

DM Ma...

MT I hear you're determined to make a stand on this new
    Food Directive. Is that right?

DM *[inaudible]* It simply doesn't hold up to thorough
    scrutiny.

MT Listen. Option One, you toe the line on the Food
    Directive. Option Two, I'll have YOU prepared for
    fucking scrutiny, you sanctimonious fucking shitpipe.
    I'll have you chopped. Blitzed. Grilled. Stacked on a
    fucking rectangular plate. Then drizzled over like a
    round-winning starter course on fucking Masterchef.

DM How dare you? This ridiculous 'Angry Bailiff' act may
    play well enough in your little Westminster boys'
    club. But I assure you it has no traction whatsoever
    in my world.

MT You simpering fucking *[inaudible, volume distortion,
    possibly 'mingebulb']*.

DM That's it, I'm kicking this upstairs. Because I think

the PM is going to support my demand for further
scrutiny. Isn't that...

MT   Oh, the scrutiny again? Where's that...[inaudible]
Right. You want thorough scrutiny? OK. What about some
thorough fucking scrutiny of your travel expenses?
Yeah, let's examine these claims made on behalf of
your 'wife'. Assuming that the slutty 22 year-old
Eurobanger who does those saucy fucking Strasbourg
hotel overnighters with you IS your wife?

*[inaudible third voice, possibly Prime Minister,
possibly 'let me have a fucking word']*

DM   Yes. She IS my wife.

MT   What?

DM   The 'slutty 22 year-old'. Marie. She's my wife. My
third, if you need to update my dossier. Hold on, Tom
wants a word. We're on speakerphone.

MT   What? Tom?

[the Prime Minister joined the conversation]

PM   Malcolm. Back the fuck off. Don's a very good friend.
He's persuaded me that we need more time to think
through this Food Directive. And I am astonished you
could use such horrible fucking language. Especially
about Marie...

*[inaudible fourth voice, possibly Marie Minchin,
possibly 'hi']*

MT   *[inaudible]*

PM   It's a poor line, Malcolm. Was that an apology?

MT   Yes.

PM   Well none of us could hear it. Could you repeat it,
please?

MT   I apologise. I was given wrong information. About
several things. By someone I shall speak to, at once.
I'm very sorry Mrs Michin. I'm sorry Mr Minchin. I'm
sorry Tom. Really.

[terminated by recipient]

* * * * * * * * * * * * * *

10 DOWNING STREET
LONDON SW1A 2AA

TRANSCRIPT *of telephone call 30.03.10, connection logged
at 13:20. Number 10, outgoing [handset B2] caller MALCOLM
TUCKER, Director of Communications. Mobile recipient: CAL
RICHARDS, Contact List status 'fucker'.*

VOICEMAIL   Leave a message. I will fuck you back as soon
            as I can.

MT   Hello you little cunt. Malc. We still on for tennis
     next Tuesday? Hope so. The PM and the rest of these
     wankers are driving me fucking demented. Sometimes
     I think we're the only sane ones left mate. Oh, and
     thank Emily for that picture of us all having a
     picnic. She sent a very sweet note with it. Just...
     just tell her I am honoured to have a rabbit named
     after me. Don't mind admitting it brought a tear to my
     eye. Gah, must be going fucking soft. Keep it oiled,
     sunshine. Later.

     [terminated by caller]

     ****

ends

DIARY PAGES

May 12 2002

PM and me in the sandpit. IP, Steve Flem, JuliusN, all
present. Tom arrived flanked by JMcL, PB and HV - carrying a
copy of the Evening Standard and a length of shelving bracket.
Tom wanted to know why the fuck JN had let Ben Swain go solo
on Newsnight re. the Britvic announcement. Tom wanted this for
himself as centre piece for his Carlisle speech.

SFlem said JMcL had okayed. PB disagreed and deliberately
knocked JN's pasta salad into recycling.

JuliusN demanded PB pay for replacement pasta. Tom said not
necessary. PM said WAS necessary. All stood. PM fronted up.
Tom began rolling up sleeves as in western. I defused by
getting Sam to bring in a crayfish wrap. JuliusN said wasn't
the same but appreciated gesture. Tom left muttering.

Bad ju-ju.

May 15 2002

French caved re NOLWAF. PM in euphoric mood. Played Jenga on
plane back. RAF best bloody guys in the world! Circled RAF
Cosford three times so I could take Dan Miller down in final
play-off.

EU looks wonky on aluminium but PM keen on throwing Cliff
Lawton for them to chew on.

Yay!

May 17 2002

All kicked off re loafers. Dan Miller from early pushing
loafers for Bradford, HARD. In with PM - I mentioned
Birkenstock mania around G8 and cooled things. But Miller,
little shit, had photoshopped PM into loafers and chinos and
JN agreed it did look good. I said could we put it on list
of options? Miller accused me of kicking loafers into long
grass and said I'd never come back re options.

Sick of this shit. Thinking of walking if we see loafers in
Bradford.

May 18 2002

Tom absolutely mental on World at One. Frothing. Said (as
agreed) it was possible PM could stay on for 10 years.
Then upped it and said he could 'envision' it (we offered
him PB to defence if he went to envisioning - cheering in
the sandpit were we). But then he added that though it was
possible and he could indeed envision it, that he 'found it
hard to conceive of envisioning it.' ??? WTF. He repeated
this phrase fourteen times under scrutiny.

I taxied to cut him off on Health stairs. Diverted him and
JMcL & PB (his bum boy) into the sandpit where we ambushed
him with JN who kept him talking UNESCO world heritage
status for fictional town of Balamoray until PM and I
arrived.

All kicked off, BIG time. Everything from last 5 years got
dragged up: Branson's golf buggy offer; the Cabbage Soup
diet NoW splash from June; PB and the battle of the golden
cricket ticket; Heath's German pyjama deal. Total shitstorm.

Tom said he would walk unless we gave him everything north
of the Wash. PM agreed and said he could also take Plymouth.
Tom also wants 8 cabinet seats, in his gift; SFlem out; and
me to sit on the Viagra story.

Deal.

Think things might be looking up. Tom and PM parted laughing
about misfortune of KL in Scotland and the end of her
marriage and personal career. Good atmosphere all-round.
Wow!

May 22 2002

Bradford.

Draft of speech from DOSAC drafted by cumsac OllieR
and old man river GC a recycled policy puke. Binned,
bollocked, rewrote.

PM arrived with Miller - in loafers. I went ballistic.
Showed PM polling on regional development and asked how
that fitted with fucking slip-ons. Miller said I was living
in a 'laced-up dream world'. I told him to jam his dick in
a bottle of Tabasco and try to bust it out by getting hard
thinking about regional development.

Miller went for me. JuliusN intervened. Miller put him in
armlock. I dislocated Nicholson's finger. Baldy out of the
picture, Miller pulled on my earlobe. I bit his cheek. PM
shouted for calm. All realised passions had boiled over.

Went for open neck shirt, suit - and, wait for it …. Lace
ups (!!!!!)

3rd lead on C4 news. Everyone very up.

Press conference 13 dead in Cyprus.

May 23 2002

Called in Steve Fleming. Asked him what he thought I had
in my drawer. He had twelve guesses. Eventually told him.
'Your fucking pecker.' Asked him what I had in my other
drawer. He no longer wanted to play. Told him, 'Your
fucking bollocks.' He wasn't getting it so asked Sam to
come in with the hessian bag I got from catering. ''I am
giving you the fucking sack Steve.' I laughed. He began
to cry. Told him there could well be a way back from this.
He brightened. I told him it was possible, I just couldn't
envision it. Big laughs from Miller, who'd come in when he
heard there was going to be an execution. What a cunt. A
sad day. But a happy one.

The Tucker Diaries
Uncorrected proof copy

Wednesday 6 April 2005

Watching Newsnight. That sultan of fuck Michael Crick was following the boss around today, doing his usual Dennis Pennis bullshit trying to get a quote on asylum seekers and how many we know are here illegally.

We don't know! No-one knows, it's currently unknowable. And that piece of shit knows we don't know, he knows we can't say we don't know and we can't say we know, 'cos we fucking don't. So thick prick-on-a-stick Crick does his fucking Paxman-lite 'yes or no prime minister, answer the question' jiggery-cuntery and we're supposed to think of him as some fucking, I don't know, soldier of truth, some fucking crusading fucking moral guardian. Jesus Christ on a Massey Ferguson.

Well, here we go then, I'll tell you a thing or two about Michael fucking Crick, shall I?

When he was at Oxford, okay, mid to late 70s he was at the same college as Angus Deayton. Yeah? The People's Fuckup. Okay, so, get this: one of the New College bedders, reliable old biddy, menopausal but sane, she told

It is our belief that the claims made against Mr Crick and Mr Deayton are unsubstantiated, libellous to both individuals, and set out to defame. Both men would almost certainly sue if such wild and obscene allegations were made public, as would the pharmacist named, and the estate of the late A. J. Ayer, and we would have no reasonable defence against such suits. This passage needs either to be excised, or substantially rewritten.

Sunday 10 April 2005

In Kent, electioneering along the highways and byways of this fine, flat, racist, nuclear-reactor filled no-cunt's land. Like the Atacama desert with Harvester restaurants and a big Halfords.

Election strategy meeting with the boss. How do we appear humble? 'Cos we're fucking not, no fucking reason to be, we're fucking brilliant at being the government. We fucking ace it, every time. But we need to look humble, wring our caps in our hands and ask politely for a third term, please, sir, to 'get the job done'.

PM fancies a curry. Nowhere open nearby, Sittingbourne is the tit-end of fuckwhere, nearest place is 15 miles away. So Colin, the runty wee fuck who looks like an off-cut from a ballbag factory, says he'll drive. PM tells him 'Go fucking fast, I'm starving. If I don't get a prawn bhuna in 20 minutes I'll fuck your nan.' So off Colin whizzes in his Nissan. Two miles away, hits a fucking deer, that's okay, on he goes, but then a mile after that, hits a massive fucking cow and wraps ████████████

Do you really intend for this episode to be put into the public domain? Were the animal deaths reported? You do realise how this will reflect on the ex-prime minister? This throws up all manner of legal difficulties and could lead to retrospective prosecutions of the former PM, yourself, Colin – it's a minefield.

Friday 6 May 2005

Okay, we're back in, reduced majority but fuck that, perfectly workable.

PM didn't sleep - full up with Red Bull, espresso, and his own maniacal air of Christ-like invincibility.

Think he's really reached it now - the TMP. Thatcher Madness Point. All long-term prime ministers get here eventually. A descent into lunacy. Proper swivel-eyed dementia. Occupational hazard. 'We did it,' he said to me at 2am. He was speaking in the first person.

Had a long talk with Mrs PM. She told me about an incident at the White House with Clinton in 1998. They'd been put in the Lincoln Bedroom on the second floor. Apparently the lock on the en-suite wasn't working. Odd, she thought, but ████████████████████████

No! No! Just – no. I'm beginning to think this is a practical joke being played on me. You CANNOT publish these words, anywhere, even on the internet. I think you need to re-assess the viability of publishing Mr Tucker's diaries at all : a good 80 to 90 per cent of this text is unusable.

Oh dear! Oh deary me – is this stuff not useable? What a massive shame. Really disappointing for you, as I made sure my contract stated clearly that my £300,000 advance is non-returnable. But, no, really – it's gutting isn't it? Best, Malcolm Tucker

March 2 2010

Crunch time for Tom, and it fucking shows. When I arrive he looks bad. Tense. Like a single gigantic fucking bruised knuckle.

For weeks the General Election has been the only story in Hackanory. But oh no, in Tom's world the Election has been The Lump That Dare Not Speak Its Weight. "Prime Minister, when will you name the day?" "Prime Minister, how much longer can this mortally wounded government limp on?" "Prime Minister, is it true you need a cortisone injection to get through FUCKING LUNCH?" Same grin, like a ventriloquist's dummy.

I give it to him straight. You think you're on the horns of a fucking dilemma but mate, the Pamplona days are over. You've got to seize the initiative. Otherwise mate, this fucking 'horned dilemma' of yours is going to gore your guts out, fuck you up the boris, then squash you to fucking bits like a meringue.

Silence. Tom looking out of the window, fossilised. Suddenly he turns round, lets out this noise like a trapped bear. Hurls his fucking Special Teapot across the room. Shards of china, fucking cold tea and dregs everywhere.

Tom just standing there shaking, staring a hole in the carpet. Fuck me, I half expect him to turn green and burst out of his fucking suit. Then, quietly: "Fuck 'em, Malc. Fuck 'em. Let's do it. If we're going off Beachy Head, we're not gonna be fucking pushed. I'm DRIVING us!"

Without warning he gives me one of his man hugs. I'm speechless. Daren't move in case he snaps one of my ribs and it punctures a fucking lung.

April 4 2010

Here we are then. The die is cast. It's been chucked up a long way, for luck. People staring after it open-mouthed, wondering where it's going to land. My bet is 'down Tom's fucking windpipe' to be honest.

Everyone's under strict orders to look Fucking Buoyant as soon as they step outside. Fatty looks like a sweaty hot air balloon covered in fucking crumbs.

Cal Richards rings for a piss-taking chat. "Mano a mano". "Mano a nano" more like, you gloaty little cunt, I tell him. If you really want to settle this in the car park, I'll fucking twat you. I'll pummel your pretty boy Rufus Wainwright pouty face into a fucking placenta. I can hear him laughing, then ringing off mid-sentence.

He's not phased. I don't blame him. He's going to be inside the fucking castle in a couple of weeks, spraying his pheromones around like some demented feral cat.

Fuck.

All we can do now is hope for a hung Parliament. And shit on the furniture.

I don't think I've ever seen Tom so happy. His face has relaxed now into the resigned bliss of someone with 24 hours to live and a steady supply of fentanyl patches.

Outside, it's the Final Battle. A fucking blizzard of last-minute spin and counterfuck. Here, in the eye of the storm, all is calm.

I watch Dimbleby doing his haughty, suave, patronising 'MC at a Freemasons' dinner' act. With the sound off. What a fucking gonk.

My new life masterplan can wait until tomorrow. I'm off to bang one out in the disabled toilet.

Somewhere in England

Mr Malcolm Tucker
10 Downing Street
London SW1A 2AA

12 June 2010

Dear Mr Tucker

I have happened upon something that I believe may be of some interest to you. Some considerable interest.

Either I, or my friend, I'm not saying which, works at the lost-property office of a large Central London railway station. I will not specify the station, as I am not a stupid man. Neither is my friend, if indeed he, or she, exists.

This Sunday a dossier of documents came into my possession. An amazing dossier. Confidential documents. Documents that could blow your government apart and bring it to its knees. I think you probably know the dossier I refer to.

Now, I am pretty sure you would like to get these documents back. I am also pretty sure that the press would love to see them. Between those two desires I spy the possibility of making some serious money.

I have a phone number for you to ring – don't try to trace it, it's a brand new pay-as-you-go phone, untraceable. If you call 07648 644788 at 8:00pm tomorrow (Wednesday), we can begin negotiations.

Yours faithfully

'Paul'

LOST PROPERTY PERVERT FOUND <u>GUILTY</u>

By our reporter

Sinclair: "I'm Robert Winston"

PAUL SINCLAIR, the lost-property perve whose disgusting sex acts shocked the nation, was told yesterday he faces a prison sentence of up to 10 years after being found guilty of gross indecency.

Shocked jurors at Southwark Crown Court heard how Sinclair:

● **INSERTED lost umbrellas into his anus**

● **MASTURBATED into an old lady's hat**

● **RUBBED his bare buttocks with briefcases, bags and satchels, and**

● **PERCHED A CHILD'S SPECTACLES on his exposed penis, shouting "I'm Professor Robert Winston!"**

Sinclair, 34, of Aylesbury Road, Walworth, had protested his innocence throughout the five-day trial, claiming he was being "set up" by "people in government" who were intent on destroying him.

But Justice Lockwood dismissed these claims, telling him: "You abused the trust of the people whose lost items you were meant to be taking care of. There are people now wearing gloves, wigs, false teeth and scarves who will be wondering whether you rubbed yourself, or discharged yourself, on their property before it was returned to them."

Sentencing was deferred for three weeks for psychiatric reports.